Lonergan, Spirituality, and the Meeting of Religions

Vernon Gregson

Foreword by Sebastian Moore

**COLLEGE THEOLOGY SOCIETY
STUDIES IN RELIGION • 2**

UNIVERSITY
PRESS OF
AMERICA

LANHAM • NEW YORK • LONDON

Copyright © 1985 by

The College Theology Society

University Press of America,® Inc.

4720 Boston Way
Lanham, MD 20706

3 Henrietta Street
London WC2E 8LU England

All rights reserved

Printed in the United States of America

Co-published by arrangement with
The College Theology Society

Library of Congress Cataloging in Publication Data

Gregson, Vernon.
   Lonergan, spirituality, and the meeting of religions.

   (College Theology Society studies in religion ; 2)
   Bibliography: p.
   Includes index.
   1. Religions. 2. Christianity and other religions.
3. Spirituality. 4. Lonergan, Bernard J. F. I. Title.
II. Series.
BL80.2.G74   1985   261.2   85-3312
ISBN 0-8191-4619-6 (alk. paper)
ISBN 0-8191-4620-X (pbk. : alk. paper)

All University Press of America books are produced on acid-free
paper which exceeds the minimum standards set by the National
Historical Publications and Records Commission.

In affectionate memory of
Bernard J. F. Lonergan, S.J.

Explorer and guide to "the eros of the human spirit"

Contents

	Contents vii
	Foreword by Sebastian Moore ix
	Editors' Preface xiii
	Preface xv
I.	**Context and Overview** 1
	The Meeting of Religions 3
	Therapy for the Theologian 10
	Religion as Spiritual Conversion 16
II.	**The Subject as Method:**
	A Therapeutic Recovery 23
	Method 23
	Levels of Consciousness 29
	Experiencing, Understanding,
	Judgment and Decision 29
	Normative Pattern 33
	Science and Human Knowing 36
	Metaphysics and Cognitional Theory 37
	Levels and Consciousness 38
	Truth and Value 41
	The Intellectual and Existential
	Desire for God 45
	Value and Feeling 49
	Community 52
	Belief 52
	Progress, Decline, Redemption 54
	Conclusion 58
III.	**Religion as Spirituality:**
	A Foundational Inquiry 59
	Religious Experience 60
	Note on Transcultural Theory 62
	General and Special Theological Categories .. 63
	Religious Interiority 67
	The Mystic 69
	Grace 72
	Spirituality 75
	Summary 77

IV. **Further Questions: Psyche, Christianity
And the History of Religions** 79
    Psyche, the Intentional Task and the Cross 80
    The Distinctiveness of Christianity 91
        "The Future of Christianity" 93
        "Faith and Beliefs". 97
        "The Response of the Jesuit" 101
        Content and Method 101
    The History of Religions and Theology 104
        The Horizon of History of Religions 105
        The Horizon of Theology 107
        The Horizon of Dialectics 110
        Dialectics and Dialogue..................... 113
    Conclusion 115
V. **Conclusion: Retrospect and Prospect**................ 117
    Notes 125
    Bibliography.................................. 141
    Index 149

Foreword

I should like to start by summarizing, very briefly indeed, Vernon Gregson's thesis as I understand it.

I cannot meet effectively with the believers of other faiths and with my own secularized world, and still less can I appreciate that my awkwardness with other faiths and with that secularized world is the same fundamental awkwardness, until I become comfortable with myself and my inner processes to a depth that is scarcely envisaged today. I have to acknowledge that my inner processes are the source of the modern world *and* are also headed to transcendence, to the same transcendence as are religious traditions profoundly different from my own, traditions which the modern world is likewise throwing into a crisis of self-appropriation, while at the same time it is throwing us together through a common technology.

To aid my reading, I have in mind an inverted triangle:

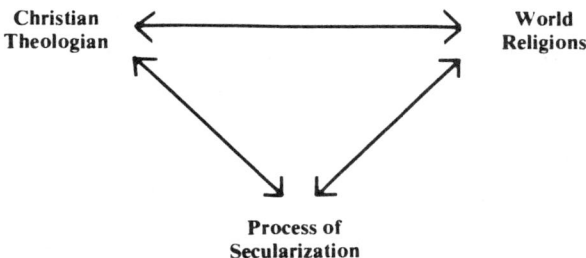

Top left is the Christian theologian: top right the world religions: at the bottom is the vastly complex process called secularization, which may be regarded as the brilliant result of an empirical method not yet generalized to take in higher and fuller reaches of mind. As a result of this only partial realization of empirical method, there is a split between those areas of consciousness where it has been realized — the scientific — and those where it has not — the moral and the religious. This split exists in the mind of the Christian theologian and in that of theologians in the other world religions. In each, it is depriving him or her of precisely that unified self-understanding without which there can be no hope of understanding the other. To this plunging of both into a common problem and plight and the consequent alienating of them from each other, we have to add the enormously potent factor of their being increasingly thrown together by an increasingly global technology, product of the same partially realized empirical method, and then we have the Gregson Triangle, with each line arrowed in both ways.

In other words, this book is eminently worth reading.

Apart from being the most creative work I know on the urgent question of Christianity and the other world religions, it is by far the best exposition I know of the basic thought of Bernard Lonergan. Lonergan is such a radical thinker that it is always possible, on reading another's explanation of his thought, to feel, "Heavens, I don't think I ever understood that before!" This happens at key points of Gregson's exposition. He has the unhurried clarity of style that only a "converted" mind can have — and we are surrounded by brilliant unconverted minds.

I would single out his exposition of the four levels of conciousness, not only because it is masterly, but because it is the linchpin of the thesis. It was in reading this, I think, that I finally parted company with faculty psychology. In passing from the level of "experience" to that of understanding, from that of understanding to that of questioning my understanding and coming to judgement, from thence to the question of value and decision, and in allowing the last level to broaden out to a being unrestrictedly in love, I am being more and more myself. Each level sublates — that is, takes up and extends — the preceding, in an intentionality that heads towards the final unrestricted being-in-love. A Christian theologian who has really, with no cheating, identified all of these levels within him or herself and the intentionality they constitute, is beginning to experience healing of the split between his secular and his religious mind, as the latter operations are now *felt* as sublating the former's. And his or her Christian religious thinking, thus newly appropriated in a univerally shared humanity, will be newly empowered to *recognize*, in culturally very different expressions, the same religiously liberated dynamic in other faiths.

There is, I repeat, a split, in the contemporary religious mind, between a very thoroughly "claimed" mind-process at the first three levels and a fourth-level-extended that, still unclaimed, is taken care of by piety and rhetoric. The pathology of this split is writ large in a widespread and rapidly spreading fundamentalism. But most academic theologians are mildly schizoid — still schizoid enough to have little to say to our scientific culture.

Also I now understand for the first time the massive nature of Lonergan's shift from the classical stance (faculty psychology and all) to the converted, religiously achieved subject. It shifts spirituality from that corner (always for me an extraordinary place for it) called mystical or ascetical or spiritual theology to the foundational position. The evidence of the mystics used to be presented in this way: "And now we have to look at some strange creatures called mystics, who *experience* the God whose revelation we are studying. You never know, you may meet one of them in the parish." The importance of this shift for world ecumenism can hardly be exaggerated. Since Buddhism and Hinduism — and the Sufi tradition — have always understood themselves as spiritualities not as dogmatic systems, the Christian theologian who is now discovering that this is true of Christianity also, has a new basis for dialogue.

The power of Gregson's intentionality-based approach is shown by the ease with which it can dispose of Jung's otherwise very understandable rejection of the traditional idea of evil as *privatio boni*. Once we realize that the self has a self-transcending intentionality, we see that the mysterious *absence* of self-transcending movement in a person or community is potentially appalling in its consequences and not difficult to recognize in the concentration camp. It is terribly unlike the absence of taste for Bach.

I would like to point to one formulation of Gregson's, at a crucial point, that improves on Lonergan's. He says, of the mystical experience, "The ultimate is mediated by the immediate experience of oneself moving to the unknown." Lonergan talks of

". . . a mediated immediacy of subjectivity reaching to God." Surely it should be "a mediat*ing* immediacy," as Gregson's formula makes clear. This is a propos of the mystic's experience, which Lonergan now holds to be the paradigm of religious or "unrestricted fourth level" consciousness. In this paradigm we see with especial clarity that, far from privatizing our understanding of religion, Lonergan's turn to the religious subject publicizes it; for it "poses the question of the relationship between religious interiority and the other preoccupations of the human subject," preoccupations that our culture hugely recognizes. To seek to understand myself as a pray-er is to enter the modern world with all its bizarre manifestations. It is also to look with new eyes at the other pray-ers who do it in ways so different from my own. I wonder, incidentally, whether Gregson would accept, as reflecting his thought, the following piece of theological shorthand: Religious belief is an interpretation of the pleasure of being without thought? I would like this to be taken with another axiom: If you don't luxuriate you don't love: if you only luxuriate, you don't love.

I would like to end on a note of gratitude for a very perceptive appreciation of my own work. I am grateful, too, for Gregson's systematic inattention (!) to what one reviewer referred to as the dishevelled character of my insights.

Sebastian Moore
Monk of Downside

Editors' Preface

The College Theology Society co-publishes **CTS STUDIES IN RELIGION** with University Press of America as part of its commitment to scholarship and effective teaching. This series presents notable contributions reflecting the traditional interests and focus of the Society including Catholic theology and life, the broader Christian tradition, and universal religious experience as well as creative teaching in college and university settings.

The Research and Publications Committee of the CTS has sole editorial responsibility for the selection, design and production of **CTS STUDIES IN RELIGION, CTS REPRINTS IN RELIGION,** and **CTS RESOURCES IN RELIGION.** Further information regarding these series can be found in the October 1983 number of the *CSR BULLETIN* and any changes will be announced there in future issues. The sale and distribution of the volumes in these three series are the responsibility of University Press of America.

The editors are grateful to the members of the Research and Publications Committee, to the officers and board of the CTS, and to the others who contributed to the editorial and production process. We also express our thanks for the personal support given by our colleagues at Marquette University and Saint Joseph's University. Special acknowledgement is made of the services rendered by Kevin McLaughlin of Saint Joseph's University Press and by Terri Boddorff of UPA.

Managing Editor	Chair, Publications Committee
Joseph F. Gower	Robert Masson
Philadelphia, PA 19131	Milwaukee, WI 53233

Preface

This study brings together three themes and a perspective. The themes are spirituality, the dialogue of religions, and the dialogue between religious and secular consciousness; the perspective is subjectivity. Spirituality and the dialogue of religions are frequently enough treated together, for spirituality is a clear meeting point of many of the world's great religions. It provides an obvious shared base for dialogue. The encounter between religious and secular, scientific, and historical consciousness also proceeds apace, but often not in concert with interreligious dialogue, for the connection between these dialogues is not apparent. I would suggest the understanding of the many levels of human consciousness which Bernard Lonergan's work brings into such clarity provides such a meeting point. The dialogues would be enriched by pursuing their mutual connection in human subjectivity. It is in that hope that this interpretive study was undertaken. I view it as an experiment in foundational theology. And I invite you the reader to explore with me the significance of religion as it encounters other aspects of human consciousness.

One of the deeper joys in completing this study is the occasion it provides for remembering. I owe a special debt of gratitude to Father Lonergan for his gracious reception of my project and for his encouragement to see it through to publication. My friends and colleagues at Marquette University provided a community of critical inquiry and personal support without which this work would have been impossible; to them I am particularly grateful: Robert Doran, Thomas Faase, Matthew Lamb, Sebastian Moore, Emily Pfizenmaier, Quentin Quesnell, Joan Schaefer and my dissertation director, W. Taylor Stevenson. I wish to acknowledge my appreciation as well to Loyola University Academic Grants Fund for providing for the typesetting of the manuscript and for the preparation of the Index; Karen Beck and Kenneth Beck diligently prepared the manuscript for publication and John Baker carefully completed the Index: to them my heartfelt thanks. I also want to thank the College Theology Society and the directors of the Studies in Religion series, Robert Masson and Joseph Gower, for their encouragement of the project and for their care in bringing it to completion.

Finally grateful acknowledgement is made for permission to include the following:

Excerpts from *Method in Theology* by Bernard Lonergan. Copyright 1972 by Bernard J.F. Lonergan. Published by Winston Press (formerly published by The Seabury Press), 430 Oak Grove, Minneapolis, MN 55403. All rights reserved. Used with permission.

"The Historian of Religions and the Theologian: Dialectics and Dialogue," originally published by Marquette University Press in *Creativity and Method*, 1981, edited by Matthew Lamb. It is included with minor changes in Chapter IV of this volume.

"The Dialogue of Religions and the Religious-Secular Dialogue: The Foundational Perspective of Bernard Lonergan," originally published in the *Journal of Ecumenical Studies*, Fall 1981. Selections are included with minor changes *passim* in this volume.

Excerpts from *Insight* by Bernard Lonergan. Copyright 1957 by The Longman Group. All rights reserved. Used by permission of Harper and Row, Publishers.

Loyola University
New Orleans, LA 70118

Chapter I
Context and Overview

In this introductory chapter I will review the present status of the dialogue among believers in the major religions. I will also identify some of the principal contributions which the foundational theology of Bernard Lonergan can make to the Christian partner in that dialogue and hopefully then to other believers. "Dialogue" I take in a broad sense. I mean therefore more than formal sessions between representatives of various traditions, though I do include that meaning. I intend the entire range of ways of taking seriously the religious horizon of the other, including person to person encounter, shared religious experience in worship and prayer, the examination of sacred literature, the study of the history of traditions and cooperation in educational, social and political arenas. My review of the dialogue, its goals and prospects is not original. Its general lineaments are shared by many: Raimundo Panikkar[1], Robley Whitson[2], William Johnston[3], Heinrich Dumoulin[4], Klaus Klostermaier[5], William Ernest Hocking[6], Bernard Lonergan[7]. All recognize the urgency of the dialogue, the potential for mutual enrichment of all partners, and the significance beyond religion of the meeting of religions. They all recognize and respect as well the delicacy of the values involved in the encounter. As a representative view I will later present Panikkar's analysis of the stages of interaction among religions and his understanding of the state of the dialogue at present.

The major focus of this chapter and of the entire study will be reserved for the reinterpretation of the foundations of Christian theology developed in the work of Bernard Lonergan. Specifically, this chapter will introduce two principal foci from his work which show signs of being seminal for Christian self-understanding and for the encounter and interpretation of other traditions. The first is the call for the recovery (and the therapeutic method for the recovery) of the theologian's own subjectivity. That subjectivity is religious, ethical, psychic and intellectual. The second focus is the delineation of the task of refounding Christian theological self-understanding, not in doctrine but in reflection on the transformed praxis which is Christian subjectivity. In a word, Lonergan calls for both the Christian theologian's and the Christian community's self-transcendence to be reflected on as foundational. Subsequent chapters of this study will provide the base in Lonergan's own thought for these elements. These chapters will also flesh out the elements and indicate the contribution they can make to the Christian theologian's task of a contemporary interpretation of the Christian tradition. It is a task no less necessary for the Christian theologian personally than for the community to which he belongs. It can also hopefully serve other communities of believers and aims, indeed, to serve the whole human family.

Hopefully in the course of the exposition it will also become clear how engagement in foundational theology, understood as reflection on spiritual conversion, is itself a manifestation of religious self-transcendence. Dialogue among religions entered into with sensitivity and discernment is a notable achievement of religious conversion. Dialogue can be seen as arising from the religious impulse itself and as a unique blossoming of it.

This introductory chapter will have three sections. The first section provides a succinct overview of the present context for the dialogue of religions. The second section introduces Bernard Lonergan's philosophical and theological method — what I will call his therapy for the theologian. This section will also indicate how that method can, and indeed must, speak to the contemporary scientific-secular context if it is to be pertinent to the religions both Western and Eastern. The third section focuses on Lonergan's understanding of religion and of theology as grounded in religious conversion — what I will call spirituality. The section will also suggest how that position can effect a renewed Christian self-understanding and provide a basis for dialogue among religious believers.

The Meeting of Religions

Let me indicate the basic context I operate from with regard to the meeting of religions. I recall the clear fact that we are in a period of escalating contact among major religious traditions of the world, in particular, Christianity, Judaism, Hinduism, Buddhism and Islam.[8] But not only is there increased contact, there is also, certainly from the Christian perspective, a new attitude of receptivity to the values of other religions. The Roman Catholic community of which I am a member has, for instance, shown a remarkable shift toward openness in this regard during and since the Second Vatican Council.[9]

It is certainly true that the western science of the history and comparison of religions has facilitated understanding about and among religions and involves in a real sense an encounter of religions. But in terms of ethical, social and religious effect, it is finally the meeting of believers as believers that is significant. For believers precisely as believers raise the further questions beyond the history of religions, the questions of living and acting.[10] It is not, then, the dialogue *about* religions, however valuable and indeed necessary that may be, but *of* religious believers that I will primarily attend to. And since among believers a special task of articulation and leadership falls to the theologians of the various traditions, I focus on the theologian.

The meeting of religions is a fact. But how is it to be understood and interpreted? What alterations are necessary in a tradition's own self-awareness because of the encounter with other traditions? The task of the theologian is to engage these questions and to develop directions which do justice both to one's own religion and to other religions. Creative reflection within each of the traditions is demanded if scholarly dialogue not only *about* the world religions but *of* the world's believers is to occur fruitfully. Theologians and spiritual leaders must face this challenge if their mission of service to their fellow believers and to a pluralistic world is to be met responsibly. In a word, theological advances, and not merely advances in the history of religions, are called for. In a fragmented world, scholarly dialogue *about* religions is inadequate, a dialogue *of* believers, all of whom are challenged by the plurality of traditions and by the economic and social crises in the modern world, is necessary.

Raimundo Panikkar has recently provided a brief typology which helpfully and accurately serves to situate the present encounter of religions.[11] Its five stages indicate basic forms of relating (or non-relating) among religious traditions. In his view, we are clearly moving toward the last of the five stages. The stages indicate the limitations and biases which characterize even the yearning for the Transcendent and the steps for the overcoming of those limitations and biases.

Isolation and Ignorance. Indifference to other cultural and religious forms characterizes this stage. Geographical isolation dictates or at least facilitates this indifference. Cultures and religions exist in self-sufficiency, although that is almost too strong a term, since the possibility of an alternative hardly arises.

Indifference and Contempt. When contact with different religions becomes inevitable, there arises first a fascination and then a disdain of the other. Defensiveness leads to an exaltation of one's own culture or religion and a haughty rejection of the rival.

Condemnation and Conquest. When contact with other religions or cultures becomes not only inevitable but even a permanent feature of daily life, a contemptuous indifference gives way to competition, a rationale for condemnation, and a move to convert and conquer the threat.

Coexistence and Communication. With time, mutual toleration and efforts at communication are seen to reap the greatest benefits for all. One rightly becomes intrigued by the balance of elements in the structure of the other's society or faith, a balance which one considered possible only in one's own way. This is a delicate period since assimilation inevitably takes place and with it the problems of fidelity to one's own tradition.

Convergence and Dialogue. After a while, convergences appear. Mutual enrichment becomes both possible and desirable. Boundaries become less rigid. "The *other* becomes the 'other' pole of ourselves."[12] There are still misunderstandings, so interpretive methodologies need to be developed. But dialogue is fact. Confrontation has become complementarity.

These stages are a typology; reality is infinitely more subtle. But the typology does highlight five rather distinct attitudes. At any one particular time, a number of these different attitudes might, of course, characterize the adherents to a particular religious tradition or culture. Panikkar's own personal history, the child of a Hindu father and a Christian mother, has made for him the dialogue with the "other" within himself, the fifth stage, almost personally obligatory for his own search for spiritual integration. The encounter is presently at that stage for only a few, although there appears little question, at least to this writer, that from the fact of the few, at least the possibility and even the desirability for the many exists. There is a caution, however. What is possible at this point for the gifted few will become not only possible but valuable for the many only through profound understanding and re-understanding of one's own tradition and culture and a comparable appreciation for the depth and breadth, religious and societal, of the other. For it would be a mistake to consider that just because some have found a personal inner dialogue[13] and integration of traditions, that the integration has taken place at a depth which really preserves and correlates the profoundest elements of the tradition, or that all relevant socio-cultural and psychological questions have been raised. For example, as profound as Ramakrishna's experiences of other founders were, the traditions of the other religions are not wholly identifiable in his integration.[14]

Panikkar, in the article cited earlier, also indicates five features of the *present* interreligious encounter, features which indicate that the fourth and fifth stages indicated above are operative today. For our purpose they suggest both the significance of the contemporary dialogue and why serious theological contribution to that dialogue is demanded. Panikkar contends that the meeting of religions is now *inevitable* since every form of socio-economic encounter obtains. It is *important* because religion in its broadest sense is the integrating factor of those who meet at other levels. It is *urgent* since the absence of a key feature in cross-cultural encounter will lead (cannot one add "has led"?) to distortion in emerging cultural forms. It is *confusing* and even dangerous since it involves the disruption and challenge of basic and deep belief-structures. And it is also *purifying* since it calls for the humility of learning from and valuing the other and of admitting that, despite claims of universality, one's own religion is not universal.[15]

I would particularly emphasize the *urgency* and *importance* of the dialogue in the meanings Panikkar gives to these words. Men and women from different branches of the human family can relate to one another creatively and redemptively in the complex levels of contemporary global interaction only through self-transcendence, through the honesty and clear vision which understands the other as he or she really is, and through the willingness to receive and to give in a way which respects the other and oneself. The overcoming of the biases which stand in the way of those attitudes, biases which pockmark the world with wars, strife and endless exploitation, demand the self-forgetfulness — really the *remembering* of man's potential — which can be named self-transcendence. And while religious traditions have no monopoly on self-transcendence, they do professedly value it and have rich resources to foster and interpret it. They are themselves in their origins and histories an integral part of mankind's interpretation and grounding of its experience and quest for self-transformation. In a word, religious traditions at their best[16] articulate and nourish those resources for human development and those attitudes of compassion and self-sacrifice in the face of evil and failure which are urgently demanded and are so frequently and evidently lacking in human commerce. The traditions are themselves challenged to the same self-transcendence in going beyond themselves, in honesty and self-forgetfulness in their dealings with each other. Only by such going beyond can they together serve the human family and their own deepest impulse to transform human subjectivity.

But there is also a further personal challenge to the religions. A common plight exists today among and within various traditions about their own self-understanding. It arises from the secular, the scientific, and the economic orientation of modern men and women. It threatens the religious with an apparent dichotomy between spiritual aspirations and other integral human aspirations. That dichotomy can lead on the part of the religion to the rejection of vast domains of the human. And, even if the domains are not rejected, the form of their integration with the spiritual is far from clear. Confusion and paralysis result. If the religions must integrate secular developments to be whole, the secular must come to integrate religious aspirations or risk triviality, manipulation and the unleashing of human greed and destructiveness. The plight then is not limited to the religions. The dichotomy also creates a crisis in the secular milieu. The secular person stands in need of the challenge and the resources of the religions both to deal with a possibly absent dimension in his or her own life, and also to act creatively, freely, and with redemptive self-sacrifice in the secular order.[17] If, then there is a dichotomy and a consequent crisis in the secular, and if religions show the shadow side of that crisis, then one of the tasks of those involved in the dialogue among religions is to search for foundations sophisticated in the understanding of the secular and of the religious and of their interrelationship. For the development in the dialogue among religions of a defensive enclave of religion would be ultimately self-defeating for religion as well as useless for humankind.[18]

A theological question in our day does not really deserve the attention of a religious person unless it is significant for more than the religious sphere. This is true of a foundational theology and a theology of religions as it is for other religious questions. This conviction grounds the choice of Bernard Lonergan's theology for this study. Of course, any theological discussion implicitly arises from and is pertinent to more than the religious context. But the contemporary need — given the dramatic split which exists between religion and the rest of human experience — is for cogent and explicit correlation of the religions with all other facets of the human enterprise. Bernard Lonergan stands toward the forefront of Christian thinkers in the boldness and explicitness of his synthesis of science, society, ethics and religion.

A process of secularization began in the West with the rise of the empirical sciences and the development of technology. Through conquest and commerce that secularization has spread to the East. Western Christianity has tried, with scant success, first to reject and then to understand secularization. Caught in the social ideal of Christendom, it could only judge the emergence of the differentiated orders of science, economics and politics as decline. Hence secularization was to be fought or fled from. Eastern religions, caught in their own worlds received scant assistance from Western religions on how to interpret this same phenomenon of secularization when it appeared in their midst. Western religion in the East in fact appeared to promote secularization and to ride on its successes. The defensive attitude of Eastern and Western religions to the challenge to their own unified social world-views hampered the reflection necessary to distinguish *the movement to differentiate* orders of reality — the order of transcendence from the physical, social, economic orders — from the consequent frequent *interpretation* that the order of transcendence was really reducible to the other orders. The differentiation might be called "secularization" and the reductionist interpretation "secularism."[19] The first, secularization, indeed presented and presents a challenge to religious men and women to expand their perspective and to give clarity to the precise character of their religious commitment. But such a challenge is not an evil but an opportunity. The failure to meet the challenge has given credence to the reductionist viewpoint of secularism that religion is indeed infantile, *pace* Marx and Freud, and should be interpreted away. That the conflicts and apparent conflicts of secularization, secularism and the social have not been resolved in any large scale fashion is only too painfully obvious. The present crisis of exponential growth brought on by secularism can, and hopefully will, provide the occasion for secular persons to recognize the realm beyond the secular and, for religious persons to enter into a critical differentiation of the liberating elements of secularization from the confinement and manipulation of secularism into which it can degenerate.[20]

A word must be added on the specific character of the crisis in Christian theology. The breakdown of the relation of religion to life which had its seeds in Galileo and Newton and the rise of scientific consciousness has only recently been taken with full seriousness by some churches, notably the Roman Catholic. Both the failure to take it seriously as well as the recent attempts to take it seriously have had devastating effects on Catholic theology.[21] An understanding that science is empirical and contingent replaced the Aristotelian conception that science concerns the necessary. In the wake of that revolution the Thomistic synthesis which was based on Aristotle became obsolete. Biblical studies, history, phenomenology, existentialism, secularization, all rushed in to provide a new basis for theology. These movements have not offered the hoped for salvation either on the religious or on the intellectual level, although the inquiries undertaken and the feedback from the results have by no means been valueless. Protestantism itself has not been notably successful in resolving the problems posed to theology by modern, notably scientific, consciousness.[22] But it has dealt with these problems more seriously and for a longer period of time than has Roman Catholicism. Its advances and studies have contributed notably to the present rich religious context and have facilitated for Roman Catholics, who have arrived late, the identification of the crucial issues. The foundation for Christian theology then, is a live question which cries for serious attention. As the breakdown of Christian theology occurred through our coming to mastery of our capacity for empirical and scientific analysis, so it might be hoped that new foundations for theology would be developed from a similar mastery of method with regard to the religious sphere. The advance which led to the breakdown of theology could be the advance which, properly appreciated, can lead to its reconstruction. In any case, the crisis in Christian theology does exist, needs attention, and will be focused on in this study from a perspective which utilizes and extends the scientific achievement that threw theology into confusion.

In the light of this briefly sketched but hopefully not misguided analysis, I suggest then that the therapeutic and methodological theology of Bernard Lonergan has a distinct contribution to make, first to the renewed Christian self-understanding preliminary to dialogue, but also to the common understanding of religious existence, the human person, and the secular which hopefully can develop through interreligious dialogue.

Therapy for the Theologian

Let me indicate the direction of Lonergan's accomplishment and say a word on how he accomplishes it. Lonergan is a theologian of the subject. He operates out of a sophisticated understanding that objectivity is the fruit of authentic subjectivity.[23] In his analysis of the human person, the subject, he uncovers the conscious operations both of our knowing and of our choosing. He discovers in the structured process of our knowing operations — our experiencing, our understanding, our judging — the same structure which when writ large operates in the human and natural sciences with their data(experiencing), their hypotheses (understanding), their verification (judging).[24] And he discovers in our choosing, both the level of ethics and the ultimate horizon of religious existence. But further, in our knowing and our choosing operating together, he uncovers the principles of the growth and decline, as well as the redemption, of the human person, human communities and societies, and also of religions.[25] If that is his theory and his vision, he hopes to share it through what can only be referred to as a therapy by which the believer-theologian becomes consciously, reflectively and methodically aware of the manifold operations of his subjectivity.[26] *Insight* initiates and invites one into that series of therapeutic exercises.

Obviously I cannot present Lonergan's entire cognitional analysis and his understanding of human choice in this introduction. But I can further indicate some characteristics which might suggest why it is to our purpose. Lonergan's theory of cognition, his answer to the question "What do we do when we know?" is not presented merely as a theory, which one might examine, compare and contrast with other theories. He does indeed present a theoretical analysis of knowing: human knowing is a self-structuring process of experiencing the data of sense and of consciousness; of attempting to understand and gain insight into the data and to formulate those insights; and of verifying or falsifying the correctness of our understanding on the basis of evidence. But besides presenting a theory, he offers in his major treatise, *Insight,* a series of carefully structured exercises to lead the serious reader to identify within his own experience each of these operations, to try to understand them, and to reflect on whether these operations are indeed his own process of knowing.

The exercise of self-identification of these processes not only provides the reader with a theory of cognition but effects a change in the knower's own consciousness. Becoming aware of one's experiencing, understanding and judging gives one the possibility of methodical control of those operations. Not that our knowing process itself changes, but awareness of the aberrations and the possible truncating of the process can facilitate our not falling into these traps. Specifically, if all of our understanding is of experience then we must be careful to amass all the relevant experience that we are trying to understand. If our judgment depends on our understanding, then we must not stop with our first bright idea but we must allow a coherent understanding to develop. And then we must conscientiously verify our understanding on the basis of evidence. Lonergan's theory of cognition is a call to a converted praxis in our knowing, including our religious knowing.

Lonergan, then, is not only a theological theorist, he is and intends to be a theological therapist also. So important is this emphasis on the identification within oneself of the elements Lonergan treats, that his work, and indirectly this study, can only be correctly appreciated in light of that goal.

Bernard Lonergan's writings have a reputation for being extraordinarily difficult. And that is not totally untrue, but not principally for the reasons one might imagine. There is, in fact, a remarkable simplicity, even elegance, to his work. But if the problem is not really, in my opinion, obscurity or even complexity, what is it? Lonergan calls for self-discovery, awareness of oneself as an operating subject, and that has not yet become painless. He is a therapist. He leads from unconsciousness into consciousness — not the unconsciousness of our feelings, but the unconsciousness of our knowing, our doing, our loving.

In psychotherapy we become aware of our feelings, name them and uncover their structure. In the therapy to which Lonergan invites us — a therapy of interiority — we become aware of our understanding and of our choosing and make their structure consciously our own. As the discovery of the pattern of our feelings liberates us in our total living, so the corresponding and complementary awareness of our intelligence, our conscience and our faith frees us to develop and integrate the often otherwise scattered efforts of our lives: our science, our ethics, our religion. Both therapies initiate a radical change in the individual undergoing them. The individual sees afresh and the new vistas which are opened up allow for integration undreamed of before.

Psychotherapy reveals the genetic stages in emotional development. Interiority therapy reveals the sequential and ever more inclusive stages of our intentionality. We admire the too rare person who has grown up psychologically healthy. But even rarer is the individual who can integrate, not just tolerate, the psychosis of Western man: technology and care; spirituality and science; institution and subjectivity.

Emotional development is gone through in full form but once, and if badly, then possibly again. The stages of interiority, according to Lonergan, are likewise cumulative; but being open-ended and heuristic, they are repeatable and repeated. Their generalized form of gathering data, forming hypotheses, and seeking verification is the basis of scientific method and indeed of all discovery of truth. But consequent upon the discovery of truth, consciousness raises concerns of value and choice, both moral and religious. Thus, according to Lonergan, the stages of consciousness provide the structure for integrating science and history into life.

Even these few words can perhaps indicate the potential theological fruitfulness of Lonergan's method. For the theologian who is aware within his own subjectivity of the cognitional principles which operate both in the sciences and in religion, has also within himself the potential solution to the alienation of religion and the secular. He discovers within himself not an alienation *from* but an identity *with* the processes which when applied to various aspects of our universe have given rise to the sciences and the consequent secularization. Likewise, the possession within his own subjectivity of the religious horizon gives to the theologian potential access to the spirituality, the religious horizon of others, and can establish a common base for dialogue.

Let me develop these points further since I am quite convinced that Lonergan's contribution to a theology of religions — which I believe to be considerable — rests not so much on the specific insights he has into the world religions or even into Christianity but on his theory and especially on his pedagogy — what I call his therapy — of the theologian's own subjectivity. For the theologian's subjectivity is the source of endless series of insights, of an endless series of theologies not only of religions but of other spheres. Lonergan's contribution is not even in providing a method for theology but in leading the theologian to the awareness of himself as method, of his own subjectivity as structuring operator.

The analogy of therapy is, I believe, a pertinent and helpful interpretative scheme for understanding Lonergan. But it is also more than an analogy. Lonergan's foundational studies are actually extensions of the insights developed in psychological therapies, therapies which developed in the context of the turn to the subject.

Psychological therapy leads to the naming of feelings operative but unrecognized in consciousness and to the liberation, control and reconstitution which comes from such identification. Lonergan's intentionality therapy leads to the naming of the cognitional, volitional and religious dimensions operative but frequently unrecognized in our consciousness and can likewise lead to the liberation, integration and reconstitution of these same operations through their identification. "My aim . . . is parallel to Carl Rogers' aim of inducing clients to advert to the feelings that they experience but do not advert to, distinguish, name, identify, recognize . . ."[27] Such rendering conscious, when the matter is spiritual experience, likewise bears more than incidental relationship to the religious exercise of discernment of spirits and of spiritual direction.[28] His interpretation of religion is largely from this standpoint of interiority and it will be examined in this context.

Although psychotherapy is a common and accepted procedure for human liberation, the need for thoroughgoing and personal cognitional analysis is as yet neither commonly understood nor accepted. And yet the crisis precipitated by the operations of human cognition and choice in science and technology is at least as serious as the personal and communal consequences of unacknowledged and unaccepted feelings.

Let me give a resume up to this point. Besides the fact that religions are in closer contact and that there is a new Christian stance of openness to the religious reality of other traditions, there is also a common dilemma both for the religious person and for secular person — or, to speak more truthfully — to the secular and to the religious in the same individual or community. It is the division of consciousness brought about in great part from the rise of scientific and historical consciousness. The dialogue among religions must take seriously this crisis whose positive features have brought the religions together and whose confusing character has led to the need for renewed self-understanding for the religious traditions themselves.

It is to this context that Bernard Lonergan speaks. He comes out of the religious context of Christianity and out of the scientific and historical consciousness of the modern world and he discovers in himself and makes available through his therapy a healing recovery of the subjectivity operative both in our religious and our scientific consciousness. In the West the fragmentation of Christian theology after the Renaissance occurred through our coming to mastery of method in empirical analysis. It might be hoped that the foundation for a renewed theology could be developed from a similar deeper mastery of method operative both in science and in religion. Such a mastery of method could also be of service to believers of the Eastern religions whose own context has been challenged by Western scientific and secular consciousness.

Lonergan's thought, then, is not only a theory but also a praxis. His analysis of human consciousness is not directed simply at understanding the human experience. It does certainly call for understanding but its goal in the final analysis is ethical, social and religious and not merely cognitional. Of particular value in Lonergan's work is that through the medium of an analysis of human consciousness he indicates how religious consciousness/experience leads to the overcoming of bias in the perception of moral values both personal and social, to the liberating of intelligence to understand the human person as maker and reformer of cultures, and to the liberation of one's freedom and goodness itself to effect historical transformation by redeeming and self-sacrificing love.

I have said that Lonergan's main contribution to a theology of religions is not to be found in his specific insights into the field but in his method for the recovery of the theologian's own subjectivity. I would now qualify that. The basic positions which flow from his understanding of the theologian's and the believer's subjectivity have quite significant consequences for a Christian and even a universalist understanding of religion. Perhaps I can best indicate this by moving from what largely have been cognitional considerations to decisional ones. For the dynamics of our consciousness move beyond questions of truth to questions of value, even of ultimate value.[29] If cognitional self-awareness is essential to the contemporary task of the theologian so that he may experience within his own consciousness the process which created the modern world and which apparently alienates us from the divine, even more necessary is his awareness of the decisional dimension of his existence, for it is at this level that he himself is religious. In addition to the cognitive levels of experiencing, understanding and judging there is in our consciousness a fourth conative level of choosing. It is the level of freedom, the level at which consciousness becomes conscience. It is the level beyond the cognitive plane of the history of religions; it is the level at which man *is* religious.

The notable differences between moral action and abandonment to mystical experience stretch this category of valuing and deciding to its limit. But both are exercises of human freedom. This fourth level is the level of religious existence, religious experience, religious conversion. It is the most radical and significant element in religion. "Religion is conversion in its preparation, in its occurrence, in its development, in its consequences, and also alas, in its incompleteness, its failures, its breakdowns, its disintegration."[30] Religious conversion is the foundation of religion. Lonergan suggests that reflection on such conversion is likewise the foundation for theology.

Religion as Spiritual Conversion

The Roman Catholic tradition has a long history of locating the foundations of theology in propositions or doctrines of faith. As a consequence its first impulse in relating to those who are not Christian is to ask, "What say you of the Christ and of His Church?" But there is a religious interiority which is preverbal and non-propositional. And it is the experiential foundation which grounds for the Christian the affirmation that Jesus is the Christ. The preverbal level is also named by the Christian tradition. It is the gift of Christ's Spirit; it is divine grace. But prior to its being named is its reality as a state.[31]

It should come as no surprise that an intentional analysis such as Lonergan's that focuses on human consciousness would locate the foundation of theology in reflection on religious consciousness, would ground theology not in reflection on doctrines but in reflection on spirituality. I will indicate some of the consequences of such a shift for a theology of religions and then further explore the grounds for the shift.

The traditions of Hinduism and Buddhism, however diverse their forms, emphasize religious existence over theory, spirituality over doctrine. For the theologian to experience and understand spirituality as foundational for Christianity and its theology is already for him to discover himself in dialogue with these major religions which are and understand themselves to be spiritualities.[32] If Lonergan is correct that spirituality rather than doctrine is the more adequate foundation for theology, then a climate for the sharing of believers of these major religious traditions is established at a level which is considered basic by all.

This new foundation for theology makes quite significant demands on the theologian. As Lonergan's cognitional therapy called for an awareness and self-possession on the part of the theologian of his knowing processes, so the consequent establishment of reflection on spiritual consciousness as foundational for theology calls the theologian to come into possession of his religious consciousness. The foundation of theology is the converted person's experience. The theologian who does foundational reflection has first of all his own experience as a religious person to draw on. His reflection on foundational reality is obviously not limited to reflection on his own converted existence. It is the *key*, however, the horizon which allows him to explore the whole range of experience which exists among those who are also converted and whose foundation is, like his own, their religious existence.

An analogy might clarify. In spiritual direction, the director need not have been gifted with or have explored all of the experience of the divine which his or her directee has received to be able to help the individual understand and integrate the experience into his life. But an individual, personally ignorant of religious consciousness, who would have to extrapolate from common experience, or especially a person hostile to religion, who experiences the psychodynamics of *ressentiment*, would be ill-suited as a spiritual director because of lack of knowledge or bias. It is similar for the theologian of foundations, for he needs some of the same sensitivity as the spiritual director. If he does not possess in himself the foundational reality of religious consciousness, he can hardly explore the dimensions of conversion without either the agony of extrapolation or a *ressentiment* unknowingly distorting his perception. Religious conversion, then, at least in an inchoate and open-ended form is a prerequisite for the foundational theologian.

> There is needed in the theologian the spiritual development that will enable him both to enter into the experience of others and to frame the terms and relations that will express that experience.[33]

Religious conversion in tandem, then, with intellectual self-awareness or conversion is essential to the foundational theologian who would address today's complex religious and social context.

In the light of Lonergan's analysis of human consciousness, he proposes a new intellectual foundation for theology. It is not a new foundation for religion. Religion is constituted by a radical change of heart, which in the Christian tradition is named God's grace through Jesus Christ. This new intellectual foundation is a reorienting of theology. As I indicated, the foundations of theology in the scholastic tradition were considered to be the basic doctrines the believing tradition holds. Lonergan elaborates the intellectual justification for a shift in focus from the statements/doctrines of believers to the believer's religious existence. It is from the horizon of faith that the statements of values and beliefs which are called doctrines flow.[34] It is in the light of this religious horizon alone that they can be understood. And the articulation of that believing horizon is the task of foundational theology.[35]

In the scholastic tradition, the articulation of religious experience takes place not in foundational theology but in ascetical and mystical theology.[36] This branch of theology was itself related to moral theology which was considered the praxis of doctrines. Lonergan is proposing a decisive shift from the theological subordination of praxis to theoria, religious experience to doctrine, to a viewpoint which discovers in religious existence the foundation for religious affirmation. Ascetical and mystical theology, then, or what is called spiritual theology, would become in altered form the foundational discipline of theology. Both religion and theology then would have the same base. Religion is, in Paul's term, the new person alive. Theology is foundationally the articulation of the new person's lived experience. The foundational reality of theology cannot adequately be propositions; rather it is persons who, living religiously, sometimes are called to formulate and affirm propositions. Such a shift by no means envisages a privatizing of religion. Rather, the shift to religious interiority is part of the larger cultural and intellectual shift to the subject begun with Descartes. Not to make the shift to religious interiority would in fact be the isolation of religion from cultural and intellectual development. To make the shift is to pose the question of the relationship between religious interiority and the other operations of the human subject. Lonergan's analysis articulates precisely that correlation.

The shift from doctrines and propositions as foundational to religious experience as foundational is not, then, an arbitrary shift from one base to another, nor was the previous base arbitrary. In the historical development of human self-understanding the fascination with the systematizing power of the mind from Socrates onward preceded the analysis of the subject himself, whose systematizing power was operating.[37] The development in this order was not without reason. Performance spontaneously and properly precedes reflection on performance.

This discovery of system-making powers ushered in a monumental advance in the development of human consciousness.

But if it certainly signaled brilliant achievements in store, its oversight of the subject led to misleading conclusions. For the oversight of the human subject bypassed the context and the confines of systematic reflection. For system is the work of subjects, and the perspective and horizon of subjects who build up systems is always finite, even when the question concerns the infinite. Subjects are historical beings.

The move from system to subject is a move from content to context, from the *achievement* to the one capable of that achievement, and also much more, if his experience, understanding and judgment are broadened. To turn from system to subject is to turn from the seemingly necessary — such as was Aristotelian science — to history, the context in which the science was formulated. For all our concepts, all our systems, have dates. And to consider the subject is to attend to those dates. The transition which Lonergan calls for, then, from doctrines to the subject who expresses them is a shift to a broader and more inclusive perspective. "The fruit of the truth must grow and mature on the tree of the subject . . ."[36] Nothing is lost in the shift of the mind's power to order and affirm. The structure and limits of its achievement, however, are better understood, and problems — such as how to interpret and evaluate conflicting systems — can be resolved more easily. Conflicting systems and doctrines are generally not to be resolved by attending to the systems themselves but to the perspective, the horizon, of the ones constructing the systems. Conflict originates there.

Both the justification and the implication of the shift Lonergan proposes demand further elaboration. That elaboration will be attempted in this study. It might be noted that the presentation will be more constructive than dialectical. I will emphasize the basis for the new foundation rather than criticize the old and will also indicate some principal consequences of the new foundation.

A further word might now be in order to indicate why Lonergan's new foundation is especially suitable for dialogue with the world religions and why a dialogue with the world religions can facilitate the development of foundational theology. If it is possible to make a generic statement about Hinduism and Buddhism, I believe it is true to say that they are best understood as spiritualities rather than as doctrinal stances. The emphasis on yoga in both Hinduism and Buddhism, the importance of the guru-disciple relationship in both traditions, the Buddha's four noble truths and the questions not tending toward edification all point in the direction of a primacy of practical and lived religious experience over theory and doctrine. This is not to deny that there are doctrinal stances in Hinduism and Buddhism, but to affirm that these religions are most profitably approached in the light of their own self-understanding as giving primacy to spirituality.

There are distinct advantages in constructing a Christian foundational theology based in spirituality in tandem with a serious encounter with religions who understand themselves in terms of religious experience, even if it were possible, in light of the dialogue already existing, to construct it separately. The reformation division of churches obscured common features among Christians, while sometimes highlighting certain second-order ecclesiastical questions. A Christian foundational theology developed solely in view of the Western context with its peculiar history of controversies might obscure the principal features of Christian religious experience. A comparison/contrast with Eastern religions forces the Christian theologian to discern and identify the values and experiences which are basic to his own religious horizon and to the community in which he lives and from which he received it. For one cannot assume one's religious values and experiences are shared by those of other religions. To discover precisely, however, how they are shared or are not shared highlights one's own foundation and provides the grounds for dialogue with those of other traditions.

Self-identity and relationship to others are not really separable matters, neither in history nor in theory. Judaism is the milieu in which the Christian church arose. Paul and Acts testify to the importance and delicacy of the disputes which led to the emergence and differentiation of Christianity. However, not only was Christianity's initial self-identity established vis-a-vis Judaism, it has not ceased to see itself as related to the Jewish tradition. As it has encountered other religions throughout history and especially as it contacts them today, Christianity's own identity and self-understanding is challenged toward development. In seeking to establish relations with other spiritual traditions, it can discover itself in a new way.

A real meeting of religions takes place in the minds of those who do history and phenomenology of religions. If these historians are also men of faith an even profounder encounter occurs, the personal transformation in the heart of a believer face to face with a manifestation of the divine. What emerges is a person fed from many sources. He cannot individually, of course, express or appreciate that encounter in a way that does justice to the depths of the various traditions of Hinduism, Buddhism and Christianity. Still, the encounter in the believer is the essential and the especially significant meeting of religions because it can release the power of redeeming and compassionate love which affects a much broader range even than the religious sphere.

Chapter II
The Subject As Method: A Therapeutic Recovery

The first chapter presented the *context* and an *overview* of this study. The context was considered in terms both of the dialogue of religions itself and of the larger dialogue of religion with the scientific and secular current of our time. The overview was a consideration of two elements of Lonergan's theology which can make contributions to the above dialogues: his therapeutic recovery of the subject and his consequent grounding of theology in the transformed horizon which is spiritual conversion. This chapter will treat of the first contribution and will present the basic elements which establish Lonergan's therapeutic intentional analysis of the subject. It will thereby provide the framework for the consideration of the second contribution: the location of spirituality as central to foundational theology. Included in this present chapter will be a treatment of method, of the levels of consciousness, of self-transcendence, and of community. A consideration of these issues concerning the structure and self-transcendence of consciousness will prepare the way for the following chapter on foundational theology, where a fuller consideration of religious self-transcendence, of religion as spiritual conversion will be presented.

Method

A frequent, if misguided, approach to method is to be so fascinated by the results of one method, e.g., geometry or the physical sciences, that one considers it to be *the* method. This approach goes as far back as Aristotle's use of mathematics as the paradigm of science. As a consequence of this tendency the method of one discipline is imposed on other disciplines. Such a prejudice is certainly operative today in the common opinion that the natural sciences and their method alone give real knowledge.[1] The further one gets from the quantifiable, the less one is dealing with knowledge. From this view, theology is certainly a discipline far removed from knowledge. Lonergan challenges that prejudice. The natural sciences yield knowledge, as do the social sciences, as do philosophy and theology. But they yield knowledge not on the paradigm of one discipline. They yield knowledge because and to the extent that the practitioners of a discipline carefully delineate the data they are attending to, understand it as thoroughly as possible, and painstakingly verify their understanding. In other words, knowledge is yielded in the various disciplines insofar as the human mind operates attentively, intelligently, reasonably and responsibly, i.e., according to its own transcendental or metamethod.[2] There is no priority to one specification of the general empirical method of human knowing over any other. Method has its operative base in the human subject. The objectivity of the results of method come not from the data, the objects investigated, but from the human subject's careful consideration of the data. Objectivity is the consequence of the proper exercise of subjectivity.

"A method is a normative pattern of recurrent and related operations yielding cumulative and progressive results."[3] With this key definition Lonergan begins his study of method in theology. As he unpacks its meaning, we discover our own consciousness in its structured acts of knowing and choosing to be the method grounding every human method, scientific, humanistic and religious. Lonergan invites the reader to gain reflective awareness of himself as method, and with that to gain insight into the operation of all methods.

But if Lonergan's work is a therapeutic recovery of oneself as method, it is conducted as a guided experiment. It calls for self-verification. In fairness to his readers and to the experiment, he calls upon them to verify, within the processes of their own consciousness, the interlocking set of cognitional operations which he names "levels of consciousness." "As a set of signs printed in a book, it can do no more than indicate the materials for a reflective grasp . . . To elicit such an act is the work the reader has to perform for himself."[4] Without self-verification the reader will find both *Insight* and *Method* "about as illuminating as a blind man finds a lecture on color."[5]

This call on Lonergan's part for self-verification is not an imperious, and perhaps even arrogant, demand of an author that one go through all of his work before passing judgment on any of it. His call to self-verification is intrinsic to taking his enterprise seriously. The personal subject is so much the focus of his concern, that heightened consciousness of one's own subjectivity is a prerequisite for adequately understanding, evaluating and profiting from his work.

Undoubtedly, there are manifold ways of heightening one's personal awareness of the structure of one's own consciousness without Lonergan or *Insight*. But unless that heightening is done, he considers one really does not have the evidence necessary to evaluate his theory properly. One should then consider his cognitional theory the results of an experiment, in the scientific sense, where acceptance or rejection rightly depends on the process of verification and the prior amassing of evidence and formation of hypotheses. Lonergan does provide in *Method* a summary of the results of his experiment, however, not to replace the labor of self-verification, but in the hope that reading them might stimulate one's interest and lead to the expenditure of the time and effort needed for such personal verification. For one who already possesses such self-consciousness, Lonergan's summary serves to familiarize him with Lonergan's terms.

Lonergan's summary presentation of his cognitional theory in *Method* and in practically every article during the last eight years can be looked upon, then, as the sharing of the conclusion of an experiment, the procedures for which are detailed in *Insight*, and the evidence for which is one's own conscious operations.

It cannot be stressed sufficiently that for Lonergan the heightened consciousness of the subject is a prerequisite both for doing cognitional theory and for being a contemporary theologian. He does not hesitate to use the word, conversion, to refer to the interior intellectual change involved in making one's cognitional processes consciously one's own.

Frequently in theology, "What is the method?" is but one question among many, but once the turn to the subject has been made, method is the key question, just as it is in the natural and human sciences. Method indicates the status of the results, facilitates their correction and development, and allows others to follow one's process. It also allows for collaboration not only with one's contemporaries but over time. Method produces not only one theology, it provides the basis for many theologies. Religion is a human phenomenon and therefore historical. Methodological contributions which respect the historical development of knowledge are then particularly valuable. Both the theologian and at least the human pole of the phenomenon he deals with are ongoing and in process.

This section on method presents the primary thrust of this study. For Lonergan's whole cognitional and volitional analysis is geared toward an individual's awareness and acceptance of his consciousness as consisting of structured methodological processes. Method is not primarily something an individual uses, method is oneself. To possess oneself is in the limit to possess the source of any and every particular operation one engages in. The significance of this claim, if it is true, and of the pedagogy to achieve its realization is obvious. And it is no less a claim that Lonergan makes. Lest it be obscure he italicizes it when he first introduces it in the "Introduction" to *Insight* and repeats it again in identical words in the last paragraph of the work 750 pages later. It is both the project and to a greater or lesser extent the accomplishment of Lonergan.

> Thoroughly understand what it is to understand, and not only will you understand the broad lines of all there is to be understood but also you will possess a fixed base, an invariant pattern, opening upon all further developments of understanding.[6]

Methodological considerations, then, are not trivial. This is particularly so in intentionality analysis. For method is not something the theologian uses, his tool: method is rather oneself. To be a methodologist, in Lonergan's sense, is not only to use one's intellegence and one's religious sensitivity in one's theology. All theologians do that. It is also to be aware of, to be consciously sensitive to, the role of one's knowing processes and one's religious experience in one's theology. Such awareness can serve as a control to locate significant questions, to avoid misleading ones, and to generate collaboration between theology and other disciplines. For the theologian as methodologist is the same conscious subject as the economist or the psychologist as methodical in his or her own field.

Matthew Lamb in his study of Dilthey and Lonergan clearly indicates a major consequence of Lonergan's challenge to the theologian to come into personal possession of his conscious operations. For to become aware in this way is to become aware of oneself as an historical being, as a being who not only lives in, but who makes history. It is also to become aware of others as co-makers of the multi-faceted dimensions of culture and to have access with them — always historically conditioned access — to the concrete and dialectical unfolding of man.

The significance of Lonergan's meta-method, it seems to me, consists in his thematisation of the basic horizon of historicality. The invitation to a self-appropriation of this basic horizon is not to reach above or behind history nor autocratically to impose some pattern on it, but to discover in one's self the open and dynamic structures of one's own constituting of history and, through collaboration with others, gradually to articulate the complications, concretizations, amplifications and differentiations of this basic horizon in the historical process itself. To appropriate the empirical, intelligent, critical and existential structures of conscious intentionality is the exact opposite of boasting an Archimedian lever that would permit one immediately to pry into all problems. For such an attitude would be an inattentive, unintelligent, uncritical and irresponsible forgetfulness of one's radical historical finitude and so evince the absence of self-appropriation. The acceptance of this historicality methodologically means adopting a moving viewpoint which, through collaboration, could work out the concrete dialectics operative in all the patterns of historical experience — whether those be common-sense, artistic, political, scientific, philosophic or religious.[7]

Lonergan's call to awareness of oneself as creator and constitutor of history through awareness of one's forms of consciousness is not a call to awareness of one's omnipotence. On the contrary, it is a challenge to be alert to and responsible for one's own historically limited and hence always finite knowledge and possibility of action, in a world of other co-makers of history and culture. But it is also to discover the connection of the forms of historical experience, a connection which seems in our own time to have come unhooked, as if religion and science, politics and philosophy, persons and institutions, belonged to different worlds.

The special methods in any particular field consist in the making specific with regard to chosen data the general principles of the human subject's meta-method: Be attentive. Be intelligent. Be reasonable. Be responsible.[8] But even before these principles are formulated, they are operative "in the spontaneous, structured dynamism of human consciousness."[9] They are operative, too, in the very formulation of the principles themselves, which are merely the articulation of the operations of our consciousness, that have been attended to intelligently, reasonably and responsibly. The existence of a meta-method in the subject's own intentionality provides the base for interdisciplinary collaboration not only among the natural sciences but among all fields where attention, intelligence, reason and responsibility are pertinent.

Divergent views on the nature and structure of human knowing and choosing, which Lonergan names "counter-positions" in contrast to his own "positions," have to be accounted for and they are, by inviting one to attend to the discrepancy between the formulations of a particular philosopher and the philosopher's own operations in creating the formulation. In *Insight*, in the section "The Dialectic of Method in Metaphysics,"[10] Lonergan indicates his view of the accomplishments as well as the oversights (the discrepancy between operation and formulation) of major Western philosophical currents: deductive methods, universal doubt, empiricism, common-sense eclecticism, Hegelian dialectic, and scientific method. Similar careful dialectical analysis will, however, be called for in terms of major Eastern intellectual traditions if Lonergan's method is to have in a clear fashion its intended universality.[11]

From these general reflections on Lonergan's understanding of method, we move to a more detailed analysis of the various interlocking stages or levels which are the methodological operations of the human subject.

Levels of Consciousness

Lonergan's understanding of religion and religious experience can be most clearly appreciated with reference to and in the context of his analysis of the stages of consciousness. Treatment of his cognitional theory will, therefore, be presented here. Lonergan perceived the same necessity for those who would read his *Method in Theology* and presents a summary of this theory in the first chapter. In fact, a basic acquaintance with his theory of the levels of consciousness is so much a prerequisite for understanding his views on religion that, as indicated above, Lonergan also gives a resume of the theory in most of his recent articles relating to religion.[12] *Insight*, however, is the primary text which establishes the base for the theory. Or more properly, one's own levels of consciousness are the primary text, which *Insight* helps one to attend to and express.

Experience, Understanding, Judgment and Decision

Humans are questioning beings. Faced with new experience, we raise questions and try to understand. We raise further questions in the attempt to confirm if our understanding is correct. Questions move us through these operations of experiencing, understanding and judging as we pursue knowledge and truth. Our experiencing, understanding and judging can be and are directed toward anything humans are capable of being aware of, sense data or the data of consciousness itself.

In our ordinary living we do not attend to the *fact* that we are experiencing, understanding or judging; rather we attend to *what* is experienced, understood or judged. For instance, one engages in the comparatively simple act of trying to put together a jigsaw puzzle or one attempts the more complicated act of interpreting a text. Ordinarily a person is only explicitly aware of the puzzle or the text, not that he or she is working on the puzzle or trying to interpret the text. One is properly occupied with the matter itself. The different cognitional operations involved, however, can also be explicitly attended to. One can be specifically conscious of the fact that sometimes he is looking at the colored pieces of the puzzle or the words before him (experiencing), sometimes he is trying to discover the patterns among the pieces or the meaning of the text (understanding), and sometimes he is considering if the visual pattern he thinks he has discovered is real or if there is confirmatory evidence to corroborate his interpretation (judging). In a word, one can become aware of one's cognitional processes. They are in fact conscious.

One can experience in oneself, then, each of the operations of experiencing, understanding and judging. One can also try to understand the characteristics of each of these operations and their relation to one another. One can, further, judge on the basis of evidence the correctness of one's understanding of one's cognitional processes.[13] To have such knowledge of one's cognitional processes is to have gained a measure of reflective control over the completeness and accuracy of one's knowing, an accuracy especially important in scholarly and scientific work. It is also to have developed a cognitional theory. After *Method*, Lonergan introduces the terms infra-structure and supra-structure respectively to refer to our conscious operations and to our reflective naming of them.[14] The infra-structure of our cognitional operations can be raised to the supra-structure of formulation.

Reference to the operations of experiencing, understanding and judging has been shorthand for the fuller sets of cognitional operations which belong to those discernably different stages or levels. Experiencing is seeing, hearing, touching, smelling, tasting. Understanding is inquiring, imagining, understanding, conceiving, formulating. Judging is reflecting, marshalling and weighing the evidence, judging.[15] Even this list from Lonergan is not meant to be exhaustive but indicative. In addition to the operations of human cognition, their sequence is also available in consciousness.[16]

Lonergan, therefore, directs our attention to our knowing processes. He discovers those processes to be conscious and their order from experiencing to understanding to judging to be spontaneous. He directs the reader in *Insight* through a series of exercises to discover these operations in himself. He invites him to experience, to understand, and to affirm the fact that he experiences, understands and judges. He invites him to acknowledge from the evidence the reader generates that his own knowing is after this pattern and with these different acts. In a word, he invites the reader to develop the reader's own answer to the question, "What do I do when I know?"

The knowledge of one's cognitional processes and the control this gives over one's operations is significant not only for the natural scientist but in all scholarly pursuits, including the work of the theologian. One can divide up tasks of gathering materials, of interpreting and evaluating them. One understands what each task contributes. Collaboration between experts in various fields is facilitated. It is premature to elaborate on the divisions Lonergan indicates for the theological enterprise but it is important to at least note here that Lonergan's cognitional analysis is directly pertinent to theology. The obvious complexity of the task of understanding and evaluating other religious traditions makes a collaborative theology particularly valuable.

Because of the nature of Lonergan's cognitional theory another element is also significant. There is a change and development in oneself as one becomes aware of and understands one's knowing processes. Not only is one's cognitional theory different before and after, there are resources and controls available that were not there before, making oneself different. This change in oneself is the primary reality the theologian uses. This is even more true when the further dimension of decision is added. For it is at the level of decision that religious existence primarily operates.

In addition to questions of knowledge, there are then questions of choice. Following questions of truth, the subject spontaneously asks questions of value. I understand the Buddhist teaching on Nirvana, but how does it challenge my own religious stance or lack of it, or the stance of my community? What is its value for me? At some point the question rises to consciousness, how does what I know challenge me? So consequent to the three levels of cognition, there is a fourth level of decision. The empirical, intellectual and rational levels of consciousness lead to the level of responsibility:

> We experience and understand and judge to become moral; to become moral practically, for our decisions affect things; to become moral interpersonally, for our decisions affect other persons; to become moral existentially, for by our decisions we constitute what we are to be.[17]

Operations on this level are deliberating, evaluating, deciding, acting, loving. It is the level of freedom; consciousness has become conscience. It is also the level on which Lonergan locates religious consciousness.[18] Morality and religion are both at the level of human decision-making. They are both freedom and responsibility in act. One must acknowledge this and also not overlook or collapse the notable differences between ethical choice and at the religious limit, mystical experience. The differences stretch this single category of valuing and deciding to its extremities. Lonergan acknowledges this when he sometimes refers to religious consciousness as a fifth level.[19] But it still must not be lost sight of that both morality and religion are interconnected in our freedom. They are the human person operating at the most personal level. The tone quality and character of the involvement differ depending on whether the response is to finite or to infinite value but they are both man at the height of his responsiveness. The interrelating of religious and moral praxis promises its own fruitfulness.

The progression of consciousness through the stages of experiencing, understanding, judging, deciding, entails increasing commitment and the establishment of who one is as a person. An individual will acknowledge that he has not understood much more readily than he will acknowledge that he has made an irresponsible decision. The latter is a personal defect, a question of character. Decision then is more deeply at the core of an individual even than understanding. The levels of consciousness then can be considered the unfolding stages of human transcendence, of human self-constitution. At the final level of decision, the subject acts to effect change in the world and by his decisions and actions further constitutes himself in his personal being.

> On the topmost level of human consciousness, the subject deliberates, evaluates, decides, controls, acts. On that level he is at once practical and existential: practical inasmuch as he is concerned with concrete courses of action; existential inasmuch as control is self-control, and the possibility of self-control entails responsibility both for what he does to others and for what he makes of himself.[20]

It is on this deepest level, this level of man's making himself, that Lonergan locates religion in its most radical and significant element, religious faith and experience, spiritual praxis.

The patterned levels of consciousness which Lonergan calls on the reader to identify within himself are not only descriptive but in a scientific sense explanatory. They form the basis for a *normative* cognitional theory for which one has the evidence to form a judgment. What that means and implies we will consider in the following section.

Normative Pattern

According to Lonergan, his cognitional theory of the levels of consciousness, although open to refinement and development, is not open to substantial revision. His expression of the theory is obviously contingent. But if the theory is the formulation of the actual processes of human consciousness, then it is properly revisable only if the processes themselves change. If the pattern Lonergan describes is the actual process of our consciousness — and Lonergan explicitly wrote *Insight* to provide the opportunity for an individual to verify or falsify this matter for himself — then any other theory would have to use the levels Lonergan formulates to prove him wrong. Revision of the theory would have to be based on other evidence which was understood differently and then judged to be correct. But this would be precisely to confirm the intentional structure of experiencing, understanding and judging that the revised theory would have been constructed to deny. And so both the right explicitation and the wrong explicitation of our conscious operations would use the same operations and therefore be evidence for Lonergan's position.

Lonergan claims then to have formulated an accurate and in the main unrevisable theory of human cognitional operations. It is a bold claim. It cannot be facilely accepted nor should it be facilely rejected. Its fruitfulness, if true, is manifest. For it would cut through the myriads of viewpoints on knowing in Western philosophical and theological history.[21] Those viewpoints would be either correct articulations of the knowing process or some aspect of it based on evidence or approximations of an accurate account, or divergent accounts in which the author failed to attend to the very processes through which he formulated his account. But Lonergan claims to have produced more than an accurate account of how Western man knows. It is an account of how man knows whether he be Western or Eastern. First, let me make clear that this is his claim before further indicating how that claim is to be understood.

> ... the argument from the cultural differences of East and West does not seem to touch our position. For while those differences are profound and manifest, they are not differences that lie within the intellectual pattern of experience.
> ... when an Easterner inquires and understands, reflects and judges, he performs the same operation as a Westerner.[22]

The claim refers to the fact of common processes rather than to the existence of a common theory. The question is not whether the Easterner (an admittedly imprecise term) either has a cognitional theory or desires to articulate one. The question is whether the Easterner's actual cognitive and creative processes include experiencing, understanding, judging, deciding. Lonergan in no place to my knowledge substantiates that claim of *de facto* universality for his position. In keeping with the experiential character of Lonergan's theory it would seem that an Easterner would have to substantiate it for himself. However, indirect evidence for the claim is readily available in the communality of the scientific quest in East and West. Lonergan's four levels of consciousness are merely the articulation of generalized empirical method. Wherever human minds operate scientifically the evidence for Lonergan's cognitional theory is present.

This study focuses on Christian foundational theology and the dialogue of religions. Traditional Christian claims of the universality of salvation available in Jesus makes evident the suitability of articulating Christian foundational theology in terms which have experiential grounding in common, cross-cultural human experience. Lonergan's intentionality analysis gives evidence of providing that base. Since that is the same base operating in the natural and human sciences, a theology articulated with reference to Lonergan's generalized empirical theory also makes possible a dialogue between religion and its greatest contemporary challengers. Lonergan's theory can facilitate the universal proclamation of the gospel and also dialogue between religion and science. Other religions understanding themselves on a cross-cultural base also achieve universality. These religions might not articulate cognitional theory, yet they are without question challenged today by the natural and human sciences and by their global effects. These religions would also stand to be enriched in their contemporary self-understanding by having available an intellectual base which was shared with the empirical and social sciences. Some such common base, whether articulated or not, is necessarily presupposed in any dialogue, whether between religion and religion or between religion and science. Lonergan articulates key elements of our common base.

In the following lengthy but careful analysis we will see precisely why his cognitional theory is in principle irreversible. Since this theory is the firm base for all that will be discussed in this study, including the formulation of the various tasks of the theologian, it is important to underline clearly Lonergan's justification for considering his position irreformable.

> . . . for it to be possible for a revision to take place certain conditions must be fulfilled. For, in the first place, any possible revision will appeal to data which the opinion under review either overlooked or misapprehended, and so any possible revision must presuppose at least an empirical level of operations. Secondly, any possible revision will offer a better explanation of the data, and so any possible revision must presuppose an intellectual level of operations. Thirdly, any possible revision will claim that the better explanation is more probable, and so any possible revision must presuppose a rational level of operations. Fourthly, a revision is not merely a possibility but an accomplished fact only as the result of a judgment of value and a decision . . . So at the root of all method there has to be presupposed a level of operations on which we evaluate and choose responsibly at least the method of our operations.
>
> It follows that there is a sense in which the objectification of the normative pattern of our conscious and intentional operations does not admit revision. The sense in question is that the activity of revising consists in such operations in accord with such a pattern, so that a revision rejecting the pattern would be rejecting itself.[23]

Lonergan's cognitional theory, then, is presented as the normative pattern of our intentional operation. He presents it as the foundational reality of all of our knowing and doing. Through it, irrevisable elements of the "eros of the human spirit" are revealed.[24] This pattern is as much the operator in our scientific knowing as in our knowing in religion and in other areas. We will attend further now to the relationship of cognitional theory to science.

Science and Human Knowing

It is not by accident that Lonergan's first three levels of consciousness bear striking resemblance to scientific methods of gathering evidence, forming hypotheses, and verifying. What modern science has writ large in its methods is indeed simply the pattern of cognition within the human subject who does science. But then, as the cognitional pattern of the human person, it is not limited only to scientific knowing, it is common to human knowing in all fields. It is the *transcendental method* or *meta-method* which is shared by all the particular methods of the human and natural sciences, theology included. It is open-endedly heuristic and since it is method, it is a recurrent process, unlimitedly repeatable. One discovery only becomes the occasion for further inquiry. The never-ending buildup of knowledge then is the natural consequence of the methodological structure of our knowing. Further methodological specification follows principally from the type of object being considered.

> Evidence in biology and in phenomenology of religion is established differently; the categories which understanding develops are different; and the methods of verification are not the same. But in each area there is evidence, categories are developed, and verification occurs.[25]

In each area there is experience, understanding and judgment. Lonergan begins his treatment of human cognition in *Insight* with an extended analysis of knowing in mathematics and the natural sciences. He chooses these disciplines because of the obvious clarity and success of their methods.[26] He also realizes that his own analysis of cognition and conation will not have credibility nor generality unless it is developed in terms of the sciences. As I have indicated earlier, it is precisely Lonergan's serious consideration of the sciences in his articulation of transcendental method that made his work of particular significance in fundamental theology and for the dialogue of religions. The way he treats the sciences is of special moment. He attends to the interiority of the scientist. The appropriation of religious interiority is a common feature of the principal religions. The appropriation of both religious and scientific interiority is not yet, however, a common feature of their theologies. Yet "theology mediates between a cultural matrix and the significance and role of a religion in that matrix."[27] Our culture focuses on both interiority and the sciences. Lonergan's genius is to link them. A contemporary theology is not possible without some such retrieval of the subjectivity operative not only in religion but also in science. Lonergan begins with the successful sciences, adds a positive critique by capturing the subjectivity of the scientist, and then reveals how that subjectivity is operative in ethics and religion. The link in human endeavors is the person who performs them.

Lonergan's cognitional theory or generalized empirical method becomes the base that was previously occupied by metaphysics in pre-critical philosophy. The turn to the subject has relocated metaphysics.

Metaphysics and Cognitional Theory

In Aristotelian and scholastic thought, metaphysics was the basic discipline. It provided the foundational terms and relations for the other sciences. For Lonergan, metaphysics is a derived discipline. It follows upon cognitional theory and cognitional theory answers the question, "What do I do when I know?" Epistemology answers, "Why is doing that knowing?" The metaphysical question, "What do I know when I do it?" is a sequel to those questions and, therefore, founded upon the answers which they elicit.[29]

Cognitional theory, then, and not metaphysics is the foundational discipline for Lonergan. The levels of consciousness of the subject reveal the methodological processes, the operating method involved in all human knowing. The cognitional theory established by reflection on all these processes provides, or can provide, not the basic terms and relations of the modern disciplines, as was the case with Aristotelian metaphysics, but the basis for the development of their methodologies.

> Former views were Aristotelian. They took for granted that the basic discipline was metaphysics and that other disciplines had to derive their basic terms and relations by adding further determinations to the basic terms and relations of metaphysics . . . the basic discipline, I believe, is not metaphysics but cognitional theory. By cognitional theory is meant, not a faculty psychology that presupposes a metaphysics, but an intentionality analysis that presupposes

the data of consciousness. From the cognitive theory there can be derived an epistemology, and from both the cognitional theory and the epistemology there can be derived a metaphysics. These three are related to all other disciplines, not by supplying them with the elements for their basic terms and relations, but by providing the nucleus for the formulation of their methods.[30]

Lonergan thus indicates the relationship between cognitional theory and the natural and human sciences. By further locating religious consciousness in regard to cognitional theory he also shows the relationship of religion to all our systems of human knowing and choosing. He therefore establishes a context for the vexing and interrelated questions of ethics, science and religion.

The contrast between an intentionality analysis of human knowledge and the metaphysical account is sharp. In cognitional theory the levels of consciousness are functionally related to one another. Each level subsumes the previous levels, which are prerequisites for its own operation. To choose the good, one must know that it is good. To know and to affirm that it is good, one must understand the experience one is concerned with. To understand the experience, one must carefully attend to it. Each level makes an essential contribution. In metaphysical psychology, one has the faculties of intellect and will, imagination and perception. The historical disputes of voluntarists versus intellectualists versus sensualists point out that questions of priority and importance are left unresolved. The arguments of faculty psychology become profitless as human intentional operations are all seen as essential and as functionally interrelated.[31]

Now that we have indicated some of the importance of Lonergan's treatment of the levels of consciousness, we will attend more specifically to his understanding of the terms *levels* and *consciousness* for they reveal aspects of his thought pertinent to our concern with religious consciousness.

Levels and Consciousness

Lonergan refers to the cognitional and volitional acts of experiencing, understanding, judging and deciding by the words *levels of consciousness*. What precisely does he mean? First, consciousness.[32] One can speak of awareness of color, or awareness of sound, or awareness of heat. There is more than the disparate *contents* of these acts, more than color, sound or heat. The contents are different yet it is not meaningless to link them together by the term awareness. This factor, over and above the object or content of certain acts, is what is referred to as consciousness. It is the factor which differentiates these acts from, for instance, the metabolism of one's cells or other internal operations of the body, about which we cannot meaningfully say we are aware. Certain acts of the human person have this common feature which we refer to as awareness or consciousness. Among these acts are the cognitional acts of experiencing, understanding, judging and deciding. Consciousness, awareness, is a quality of these acts. It is not their object, for these objects are quite dissimilar, but it is an element or component of the acts. And it is not meaningless to say that it is a *common* component; a component integral to the acts.

One can also *attend* to the conscious acts one is performing. From experiencing color, one can attend to the fact that one is experiencing color. From deciding, one can attend to the fact that one is deciding. That shift does make consciousness explicit, does heighten it; but the act of making one's cognitional or volitional acts the object of consciousness, does not constitute consciousness and is not the normal state of consciousness. Consciousness is immanent in our normal acts of knowing, even if it is only on specifically attending to those acts that we become explicitly aware that they are in fact conscious.

In addition, the character of our consciousness is not uniform.[33] Its quality changes as the intentional acts we perform change. As we move from experiencing to understanding to judging to deciding, it is a fuller subjectivity which is operating and hence present to itself. Lonergan refers to this unfolding of our consciousness by the term *levels*. As experientially conscious, we are basically operating at the level of the higher animals. This level is the substratum for the further operations, just as each succeeding level and what has gone before it is substratum for the next level. Our experience calls forth our desire to understand. We search for relatedness within the data and between data; we are intellectually conscious. A fuller subjectivity, a more exclusively human consciousness, is operating here than at the empirical level. But in addition to and building on the empirical and intellectual level there is rational consciousness. This is the level at which we judge our understanding. Experience and understanding are presupposed and a fuller self asks if our understanding is correct. We take a critical stance toward our own inquiries. We are present to ourselves as seeking truth. But there is even a further dimension to being human. Besides seeking truth, we can pursue value. In addition to knowing the truth, we can do it. We move into full human subjectivity when our consciousness, building upon experience, understanding and judgment, becomes decisional.

The move to full selfhood is an unfolding development of different but interrelated types of conscious acts. We are not fully human when our self-presence is merely as experientially alert; though without experiential awareness, we cannot be present to ourselves as questioning and understanding. There would be nothing to understand. We are not fully human, however, even when we are alert as inquirers; though without intelligent questioning we cannot be present to ourselves as critically reflecting on our understanding. There would be nothing to reflect upon. We are not full persons, however, even when we are present to ourselves as critically seeking the truth; though without the knowledge which judging gives there would be no field in which to be decisional. We become full persons only as present to ourselves as making our world by our choices, and making ourselves by the quality of our choices. We are fully human in our self-presence as valuing and as allowing ourselves to be valued, in being loved and in loving.[34]

These reflections on Lonergan's understanding of the levels of human consciousness pertain to the central core of his contribution to a foundational theology of religions. Lonergan's therapy for the theologian is precisely the uncovering and identifying of these forms of self-presence within the theologian himself. Their identification leads to the theologian's deeper attunedness to his own interiority. In identifying within himself the experiential, intellectual and rational forms of consciousness, the theologian discovers also his at-one-ness with his brothers and sisters who direct their consciousness at these levels to the data of sense and develop the natural sciences. The theologian is challenged by the success of the natural sciences to discover how these conscious operations operate within his own discipline. Lonergan's delineation of the tasks of the theologian, what he calls functional specialties, is his own articulation of how the theologian's forms of consciousness establish his discipline, just as those same conscious operations establish the structure of the disciplines of the other sciences, natural and human.

Before we further explore the tasks of the theologian, however, it will be necessary to discuss in some detail the particular nature of religious consciousness. Pertinent to that discussion are the matters of value and feeling, elements which are integral to the highest level of self-transcendence. We begin by relating valuing to the three preceding levels whose goal is truth.

Truth and Value

All of our questions for understanding and reflection intend truth. The desire for truth leads us through our inquiries and is unsatisfied with every incomplete understanding. Yet it also invites and even compels assent when there is sufficient evidence for our hypothesis. This desire for truth leads to the self-transcendence of affirmation that this or that is really so. It is the dynamism which leads us from experiential to intellectual to rational consciousness. Lonergan refers to this dynamism toward truth as the transcendental notion of truth. It is a *transcendental* notion since it motivates and guides *all* our inquiries.

> It is the absorption of investigation, the joy of discovery, the assurance of judgment, the modesty of limited knowledge. It is the restless serenity, the unhurried determination, the imperturbable desire of question following appositively on question in the genesis of truth.[35]

But in addition to the transcendental notion of truth, there is the transcendental notion of the good, of value. It is the dynamism which leads our consciousness beyond the cognitional to the existential. Like the cognitional dissatisfaction with all incomplete understanding and falsehood, there is existential dissatisfaction with all that is sham. It moves beyond the element of pleasure or pain to the element of what is really worthwhile. And in the choice of value, the subject not only chooses the good, he becomes good, just as with the attainment of truth, the subject achieves personal self-transcendence in truthfulness. The decision for value leads not only to the creation or fostering of value but to the making of oneself as a moral person. By our choices we ourselves "can be principles of benevolence and beneficence, capable of genuine collaboration and of true love."[36] We are "originating values."[37] This is no work of the moment. As one truthful statement does not make one trustworthy, so one choice of value does not make one virtuous.

But if there is faltering on the part of the subject, there is also limitation to the value of objects. The transcendental notion of value seeks for value beyond all power of criticism, just as the dynamism of the notion of truth pushes toward complete intelligibility and truth. The intentionality of value brings to light the limitations of every finite achievement, reveals the contrast between our desires and our performance.

> It plunges us into the height and depth of love, but it also keeps us aware of how much our loving falls short of its aim. In brief the transcendental notion of the good so invites, presses, harries us, that we could rest only in an encounter with a goodness completely beyond its powers of criticism.[38]

The orientation of our consciousness toward value is what drives us toward the transcendent. Lonergan's delineation of this notion of value provides the anthropological base in his intentionality analysis for the transcultural search for the Absolute. It is his key general theological category.[39] The desire for absolute value can only find its rest in the Absolute. The dynamism of the notion of value likewise grounds Lonergan's understanding of the mystic as one who "drops the constructs of culture" and returns to "a new, mediated immediacy of his subjectivity reaching for God."[40] The notion of value is central to Lonergan's understanding of *homo naturaliter religiosus*.

Lonergan's understanding of value in *Method in Theology* is a distinct advance over his treatment of value, the good, in *Insight*.[41] There the good was the intelligible and the reasonable, and moral decision was bringing choice to conform to knowledge. In *Method*, however, the good is a proper notion, distinct from the intelligible and the reasonable.[42] It is what is specifically intended in those special questions which we call existential or deliberative. This shift to a distinct intentional notion of value also grounds, in my opinion, Lonergan's shift from the priority he gives to the proof for God's existence in *Insight* to the central role of religious experience in *Method*. The broadening of intentionality from the intelligible to the valuable is paralleled by the shift from argument to worship. In any case, if one is to deal with religion in its full scope, then the necessary anthropological ground for doing that is the intentionality found in the notion of value.

As there are judgments of fact whose criterion is the cognitionally self-transcending subject, so there are judgments of value whose criterion is the volitionally self-transcending subject. In both cases the person affirms that something is objectively so or something is objectively good independent of the whim of the subject. Full moral self-transcendence, however, demands more than the judgment of value. One can know what is good but not choose it. Not only knowledge but praxis is necessary for full selfhood.

The progression in consciousness through the stages of experiencing, understanding, judging and deciding-acting unfolds the stages of human self-transcendence. In *Insight* Lonergan described the dynamic structure of human consciousness, this drive toward transcendence, primarily in its cognitional dimensions. He named it, "the pure, disinterested desire to know."[43] It is a primordial orientation and could be described as pure question. It is Aristotle's wonder. It is the exigence which leads one from level to level of consciousness. It is open-ended. It can and does inquire and raise questions about anything and everything.[44] All matters of truth, of value, and of God are in principle within its horizon. Lonergan's recent correction of the context for Chapter 19 of *Insight* on God[45] is not a repudiation of the view that the question of God is within man's horizon. Rather it is a recognition that the question is in fact almost universally raised in its intellectual form only subsequent to religious experience and not prior to or independent of such experience.

The self-transcendence which is the goal of the dynamism of consciousness reaches its highest point, though, not in the cognitional self-transcendence of true judgments — even true judgments about God — but in decision and action: the moral orientation to value and the religious surrender to the Ultimate. Moral self-transcendence is achieved, however fragilely, whenever values are chosen rather than satisfactions. Kierkegaard's distinction between the ethical and the aesthetic man hits the difference off well.[46] Experience, understanding and judgment, when given free rein in their own sphere of transcendence, present for deliberation what is truly good and not merely what avoids pain or is for our pleasure.[47] To live with moral authenticity is to live at, and be concerned with the level of value: the values of life and health, of family and society, of art and science, of one's own development and the development of others. It means one has to move beyond selfishness to the manifold varieties of the good: to the realm of vital, social, cultural and personal values. In *Method*, Lonergan delineates the elements of both the individual and the social construction of value. It is important to note that self-transcendence is not a privatized achievement. In fact, it is achieved precisely by the quality of choices of meaning and value by which, with others, one constitutes the world.[48] The subject acts to effect change in the world and by his action and the decision which precedes it, constitutes himself in his moral being. He or she has become existentially and practically self-transcendent.[49]

The achievement of self-transcendence is the way the human person achieves authenticity.[50] But besides authenticity, there is inauthenticity. Self-transcendence is always precarious. The striving for truth, value and the Ultimate can be perverted through false judgments and evil decisions. There is a dialectical character to human self-transcendence. The fragile state of moral self-transcendence, however, receives stability if grounded in love, if grounded in stable affectivity. Love is self-surrender to value. When present, it becomes the principle of action and makes easy the discernment of what is good. The forms of love at the level of self-transcendence are manifold: the love of intimacy with spouse and children; the love of one's friends, one's fellow man, one's country, one's neighbor. Love transforms moral self-transcendence from being a single act or even a series of acts and makes it a dynamic state which affects everything in its purview.[51]

To love of the finite, one can add love of the Infinite. One can fall in love with God. Moral self-trancendence becomes religious self-transcendence. Distinctions will later have to be introduced which pertain to those religious traditions which do not refer to religious self-transcendence in terms of God and of love. The many facets of religious experience will begin to occupy us in the following section. What we will point out here is that, for Lonergan, religious self-transcendence is the fulfillment of ultimate human questions of our conscious intentionality: "... as unrestricted questioning is our capacity for self-transcendence, so being in love in an unrestricted fashion is the proper fulfillment of that capacity."[52] Consciousness at this level can be broadened, deepened and enriched but it can never be surpassed. The self-transcendence which begins with experiential consciousness, reaches its culmination in religious consciousness.

The capacity of man for God, particularly as revealed in the open-endedness of his capacity to question, receives detailed analysis in Lonergan. We present now in some depth his exposition of the human person as questioner, as desirer of knowledge and value, even ultimate value. It is the basic context for what is finally the fulfillment of desire, the experience of the Ultimate.

The Intellectual and Existential Desire for God

Questioning is what moves man up the cognitional-volitional ladder from experience to understanding, to judgment, to decision. It is founded in a "deep-set wonder" in which "all questions have their source and ground." "Man's artistry testifies" to the "elemental sweep" of this wonder.[53] Wonder and its consequent questioning is unrestricted. We have studied human questioning as it develops through the levels of consciousness. We will attend here to two aspects of that questioning as it pertains to the Ultimate. First, how and in what context does the intellectual question of the existence and nature of God arise? Here we will treat of what have classically been called the proofs for the existence of God. We will show how Lonergan presents the intellectual question in terms of intentionality analysis. We will also see a change in Lonergan's own understanding of the context for raising the intellectual question of

God. This will lead to a treatment of a second existential aspect of the desire for God.

Lonergan reflects systematically on man's unlimited desire to question and specifically on his capacity to raise questions of ultimate meaning, questions about an absolute. Man may not attain the absolute but there is in his experience this intending of an ultimate, the question about ultimate value. This questioning opens up the region of the divine from within our human experience, even if some would declare the region empty. Even an ultimate denial of the divine supposes "the spark in our clod"[54] which can entertain the reality of God.

In his brief book, *The Philosophy of God, and Theology,* Bernard Lonergan acknowledges that a significant revision is necessary if the question of the existence of God presented in his major treatise, *Insight,* is to be properly situated. His exposition in *Insight* does not attend to the full experiential perspective of the individual considering the question of God.[55] The awareness of God, he now contends, generally precedes any intellectual consideration of his existence and nature. "Only secondarily do there arise the questions of God's existence and nature, and they are questions either of the lover seeking to know him or of the unbeliever seeking to escape him."[56] Lonergan's proof of God's existence in *Insight* is not founded in or related to that surrender of faith or the fending off of that surrender.

The disembodied approach to the question of God in *Insight* is not consistent with the experientially grounded cognitional theory developed in the earlier sections of *Insight* nor with the clear direction of Lonergan's thought after *Insight*. Disincarnate objectivity is a deception. Rather objectivity is achieved precisely when a person operates out of his or her full resources as a human subject. One should understand "objectivity to be the fruit of authentic subjectivity."[57]

Lonergan's recantation of the context, if not the content, of his presentation of God in *Insight* is welcome, even if not surprising, in the light of his post-*Insight* theological focus. For if providing the experiential base for cognitional theory is a primary concern in *Insight*, establishing the experiential base for religion is a key emphasis in his more recent work culminating in *Method in*

Theology.

In *Method*, Lonergan presents three forms of the question of God that flow from an analysis of man's knowing and choosing. First, our attempts to understand our universe imply that the universe is intelligible. Could this be if there were no intelligent ground to our world? Second, we judge a statement true if the conditions upon which it depends have been grasped as fulfilled. Is there a being whose reality has no conditions whatsoever? Third, we deliberate about whether something is valuable or not. Are we the final source of valuing in our universe or is there an ultimate instance of moral consciousness who gives final meaning to our valuing?

> Could the world be mediated by questions for intelligence if it did not have an intelligent ground? Could the world's facticity be reconciled with its intelligibility, if it did not have a necessary ground? Is it with man that morality emerges in the universe so that the universe is amoral and alien to man, or is the ground of the universe a moral being?[56]

All three questions arise from who we are and the reflective acts that we engage in. Our own reality, then, as we experience and live it raises the question of God. Our understanding of ourselves places us on the brink of this transcendent question. It is not a peripheral matter but central to our basic cognitional and volitional operations. "Man's transcendental subjectivity is mutilated or abolished, unless he is stretching forth towards the intelligible, the unconditioned, the good of value."[59]

The forms of the questions are as varied as men and times and cultures are varied. But beneath such "differences of manifestation and expression," of "alien elements that overlay, obscure, distort," at the "root there is the same transcendental tendency of the human spirit that questions, that questions without restriction, that questions the significance of its own questioning, and so comes to the question of God."[60]

But in addition to the question of God which arises from the search for a ground for man's understanding, judging and valuing, there is a further, a more common, and a more existential questioning of God. It arises from man's experience of evil both within himself, within others, and within his world. It is an experience of man's existential helplessness which cries out for judgments of value do not exist in isolation but in contexts of growth or decline, personal and communal. We will attend briefly to those contexts before focusing on feeling. In growth, one's knowledge increases in scope and precision and one's valuing moves away from sense satisfaction to the realms of vital, social, cultural, personal and religious living. It is only finally, however, in the valuing of the Transcendent that the grounding of all other values is secured. In Christian terms, when one's supreme value is God, all other values are seen as the expression of God's love in this world. In the light of valuing the Transcendent, all other values find their place. And Augustine's phrase becomes true, *Ama Deum et fac quod vis.*[68] If one loves God, then what one desires will be value and what one hates, evil.

But this is only an "ideal type" of growth. There are indeed communities of growth as there are individuals of extraordinary stature. But for most, development is neither complete nor sustained. So one can develop an "ideal type" of decline. Settled routines hold sway. Higher values are ridiculed or ignored. "Bias creeps into one's outlook, rationalization into one's morals, ideology into one's thoughts."[69] Individuals, groups and nations can destroy themselves or others when the intentionality of value is rejected, when value feelings become perverted. The trajectories of growth and decline permit us to see the height and depth of human possibility, of human feeling and human choice. These possibilities are cross-cultural since they are based on the directionality of consciousness by which we define the human. The particular constellation of possibilities varies from age to age, from culture to culture, but the range of values pertain to similar concerns, the vital, the social, the cultural, the personal, the religious.

Lonergan is dependent on Dietrich von Hildebrand for his treatment of feelings.[70] Von Hildebrand indicates two classes of feelings. First, there are non-intentional states and trends. Examples of states are fatigue, irritability, anxiety. Experiencing them, we look for their cause. Examples of trends are hunger, thirst, sexual desire. Experiencing them, we look not for their cause but for what will satisfy them; we look for their goal. Our feelings then precede our search or our apprehension of either their cause or their goal. We are anxious and look for the cause; we are hungry and look for food. Secondly, however, there are intentional feelings. They presuppose and respond to a perceived object. They relate us to persons and objects. They give to our consciousness its flesh and its substance. They are the mass and momentum of its dynamism. Lonergan calls our knowing and deciding "paper thin"[71] if it is without feeling. We not only know and do, we desire and fear, hope and despair, rejoice and are sorrowful, love and hate, dread and revere. Our feelings orient us dynamically and forcefully to the real. Our feelings are for and with other persons, are about situations and things. Feelings express the "passionateness of being," its "color and tone and power."[72]

There are two main aspects of objects which intentional feelings regard: the agreeable and disagreeable, value and disvalue. Response to value, to persons, beauty, truth, understanding, virtue, all lead to self-transcendence, to our further becoming as persons. Response to pleasure and pain is ambiguous. What is good might be pleasurable but it might also be painful. The choice of value often includes decisions which involve suffering as well as delight.

The values we respond to are not all on the same level. Lonergan lists the following ascending classes of values. Vital values, such as health and strength; social values, such as the good of order, which provide vital values for the community; cultural values, such as the expression of meaning and beauty, which build on vital and social values; personal value, the person himself as lover and loved, as originator of values; religious values, the Transcendent itself, our worship and our being ultimately loved.

By our discussion of value we have set the stage for a discussion of community. For it is at the level of value that the interpersonal takes on its full significance.[73] Community is the context of Lonergan's work and of this study. It is in the context of a historical community of shared understanding and belief that Lonergan is able to articulate the dimensions of self-transcendence which ground or destroy community and the communal dimensions which facilitate or undermine personal self-transcendence.[74] It is in the historical context of possible world-community that a discussion of the meeting or religions is both possible and pertinent.

Community

The cognitional theory of levels of consciousness provides the basic terms for Lonergan's understanding of community. Community is clearly a pivotal element in any study of religion,[75] and it is so for Lonergan. The levels of consciousness are not only levels of personal process, they also constitute fundamental stages of community development. In so far as there is shared experience, understanding, judgment and allegiance, community exists. Common experience provides the possibility of community. If that experience is commonly interpreted, community has begun to form. If that experience is differently interpreted, rival communities form. Since experiences and their interpretations are manifold, there is the possibility and the fact of intersecting communities: communities of morals and religion, art and literature, economics and government, science and philosophy.[76]

Lonergan distinguishes between what he calls lower and higher cultures on the basis of their ability to *control* meaning.[77] All culture has moved beyond the child's world of sensible immediacy to a world where image, word, and symbol mediate the absent, the past, the present, the future, the possible. Lower cultures live in the world mediated by meaning, but lack the control of those meanings and are hence prone to magic. Higher cultures do have controls of meaning through alphabets, dictionaries, logics, rhetorics, etc., but are themselves divided between those which conceive controls as fixed for all times (the classical) and those which discover the controls themselves to be in process (the modern). The stages of meaning and their control then permit the differentiation of cultural development. Similar to the stages of cultural development are the stages of individual development from the immediacy of childhood to the mediation and control of the world through meaning.[78]

Belief

Lonergan examines the social and historical character of human knowledge, what sociologists call the sociology of knowledge. There is certainly much that one finds out for oneself, from one's own experience, insights and judgments of fact and value. But reflection indicates how small a part one's own personally generated knowledge is in one's whole store of knowledge. One's knowledge is enriched by the discoveries of family and friends, of teachers and researchers, of fellow citizens and those of other nations. And they, too, stand in a historical stream whose source we cannot trace. Even much of the knowledge we personally come to is merely the repeating of insights and discoveries made by others. "Not only are men born with a native drive to inquire and understand; they are born into a community that possesses a common fund of tested answers, and from that fund each may draw his variable share, measured by his capacity, his interests, and his energy."[79]

The natural sciences, which of all areas would most appear to be a matter of knowledge rather than of belief, are actually collaborations of believers. Scientists do not spend their lives redoing each other's experiments. The advancement of science precisely demands a division of labor. Original scientific discovery is a matter of immanently generated knowledge, but even here much that is pertinent to innovative research is received from the work of others and is therefore only indirectly verified, even by the innovator. The indirect verification of scientific hypotheses through their use in contexts where they are assumed is key to the building up and the confirmation of a field of research. Unlike the initial direct confirmation, indirect confirmation has the strength of discovering the suppositions and consequences of the discovery in a continuous and cumulative manner.

> Nor is this all, for empirical science is a collective enterprise to so radical an extent that no scientist can have immanently generated knowledge of the evidence that really counts; for the evidence that really counts for any theory or hypothesis is the common testimony of all scientists that the implications of the theory or hypothesis have been verified in their separate and diverse investigations. In plainer language, the evidence that really counts is the evidence for a belief.[80]

Indirect confirmation and falsification in the sciences is the same process operative in our beliefs from other quarters. We do not doubt everything, as in Descartes' proposal, and then try personally to prove it. Rather we believe, as Newman suggests,[81] and let mistaken beliefs reveal themselves in the operations of living. Then they can be reversed in the light of the evidence which proves them false. To operate consistently any other way would place us with our prelinguistic ancestors without even the tools for doubt or for verification.

When error is discovered, one tries to uncover other related views which supported it. They too might be errors. One error can lead to the unmasking of other mistakes. But in addition to mistaken beliefs, there is the mistaken believer. Erroneous belief can lead to the discovery of the bias or carelessness of the believer and call for a shift in his own viewpoint, even a conversion to a new perspective. There is then a self-corrective process of learning in which mistaken beliefs make for their own undoing as they are lived out.[82]

Progress, Decline, Redemption

Progress or creativity in history arises through the cumulative and cooperative unfolding of the stages of human self-transcendence.[83] Progress in society begins with subjects, subjects faithful to the dynamism of their desire for truth and value; subjects faithful to the precepts: be attentive, be intelligent, be reasonable, be responsible; subjects attentive to the society in which they live, persons who, living authentically, grasp new possibilities, reasonably discard those possibilities that probably will not work and adopt and commit themselves with others to courses of action which bring real benefit to themselves and to others. The transcendental precepts are a permanent legacy and continue to operate in the new situation, spotting oversights in what has occurred and discovering possibilities to correct them. The changes themselves will have opened up the possibility of other changes. So change begets change and sustained cumulative changes are what constitute progress.

> For concrete situations give rise to insights which issue into policies and courses of action. Action transforms the existing situation to give rise to further insights, better policies, more effective courses of action. It follows that if insight occurs, it keeps recurring; and at each recurrence knowledge develops, action increases its scope, and situations improve.[84]

Problems are identified and understood. Solutions are investigated, evaluated, chosen and effected. In creating the world, men and women create themselves as moral persons. But human history is not merely the record of human progress. Besides obedience to the transcendental precepts, there is the incidental or systematic disregard of them. In place of the dynamic of progress there is the dynamic of decline; "inattention, obtuseness, unreasonableness, irresponsibility produce objectively absurd situations."[65] If creativity establishes policies and contexts which facilitate development, decline produces objective absurdities which block and discredit the insights or actions which could reverse the trend. Alienating situations effect further alienation. The source of this alienation, what might be named "the basic form of alienation"[66] is men and women's disregard for the transcendental precepts of their own self-transcendence.

Lonergan develops at length four particularly prevalent forms of alienation or bias.[67] There is the psychic bias of the neurotic who flees insight into affect. There is the individual bias of the egoist who chooses those insights which lead to personal advantage. There is the group bias of collective egoism which sets up privilege and rejects insights which would lead to its own transformation. There is lastly the general bias of the common sense man or woman which rejects the probing insights of theory as idle nonsense. Bias blocks the unfolding of personal and social human growth. Bias blocks creativity and progress.

Although Lonergan pinpoints the recurrent forms of bias at the levels of insight and at the more basic level of experience which one refuses to attend to, he does not discover the *root* of bias to be at the level of its manifestation. The cognitive process is blocked at the volitional level. One is only willing to attend to and to understand what one is willing to accept and to choose. The higher, fourth level, antecedent willingness or unwillingness to respond to value, or to create it, effectively constricts one's capacity to understand. One's "rational *self*-consciousness" — Lonergan's terms in *Insight* for fourth level questions — inhibits one's "intellectual" and "rational consciousness." "For unless one's antecedent willingness has the height and breadth and depth of the unrestricted desire to know, the emergence of rational self-consciousness involves the addition of a restriction upon one's effective freedom."[88]

Progress and creativity involve ever more inclusive and collaborative experience, understanding, judging and praxis. Effective unwillingness blocks this upward move through man's cognitive functions and brings in its wake decline. Only a transformation of man's willingness, a healing at his core can release again the energies of creativity. A healing at the existential level of man's being is demanded if decline is to be offset and reversed. The transformation of willingness which is religious conversion heals at the root the source of decline. Opening man's horizon to Ultimate Value, it leads to response to the realm of finite value which is moral self-transcendence. Moral conversion liberates man's willingness and so hits at the root of the bias of his understanding. How the transformation of willingness which is spiritual conversion takes place, how men and women are healed at this level is variously interpreted by the world's religious traditions. *That transformation*, at the level at which one loves the Ultimate, is what Lonergan locates at the core of religion. Religion heals men and women at the center of their interiority and leads to healing and the release of creativity at the moral, intellectual and psychic levels.

> For human development is of two quite different kinds. There is development from below upwards, from experience to growing understanding, from growing understanding to balanced judgment, from balanced judgment to fruitful courses of action, and from fruitful courses of action to the new situations that call forth further understanding, profounder judgment, richer courses of action.
>
> But there is also development from above downwards. There is the transformation of falling in love: the domestic love of the family; the human love of one's tribe, one's city, one's country, mankind; the divine love that orientates man in his cosmos and expresses itself in his worship. Where hatred only sees evil, love reveals values . . . Where hatred reinforces bias, love dissolves it, whether it be the bias of unconscious motivation, the bias of individual or group egoism, or the bias of omnicompetent, short-sighted common sense. Where hatred plods around in ever narrow vicious circles, love breaks the bonds of psychological and social determinism with the conviction of faith and the power of hope.[89]

The world in which we live corresponds neither to the trajectory of progress nor to the trajectory of decline. Rather with the reality of personal and communal religious self-transcendence, the redemptive power of compassion and love is operative. Lonergan's analysis of progress, decline and healing in individuals and in communities is consistent with and follows from his understanding of the levels of human interiority. Religion is located as the ultimate transforming force in human society. Lonergan is precise, then, on the social function of religion. It overcomes man's personal and social impotence before the evil which he effects and which he inherits. The ultimate moment of religion is, indeed, private but not privatizing. If Lonergan's analysis is accurate then religion is not merely what one does with one's solitude.[90] Rather, the character of one's solitude indicates how one heals and creates in history.

Lonergan, then, analyzes the structure of progress and decline in society. He does this to locate the precise point at which religious love and compassion affect the social order. His analysis provides the basis for his position that religious transformation leads to moral transformation which in turn leads to intellectual transformation. He observes that

> from a causal viewpoint, one would say that first there is God's gift of his love. Next, the eye of this love reveals values in their splendor, while the strength of this love brings about their realization, and that is moral conversion. Finally, among the values discerned by the eye of love is the value of believing the truths taught by the religious tradition, and in such tradition and belief are the seeds of intellectual conversion.[91]

Crises in personal and social experience focus on the need for liberating power. Religious liberation empowers the overcoming of evil and its reversal with good. Again what is particularly significant for our purposes is the heuristic, intentional nature of Lonergan's analysis. An intentional base is cross-cultural and hence relevant in the comparison of traditions and for the discovery of the function of religion in any society.

Conclusion

Lonergan's first and most basic contribution to theology is his therapeutic recovery of the subject. Through *Insight* he invites the believer-theologian to a fuller possession of himself in his cognitional and volitional consciousness. Such recovery of the theologian's own subjectivity permits him to move beyond the split of science and religion-ethics, which has created and ever threatens to destroy the modern world, to a retrieval of the methodological operations of consciousness which operate in all spheres of the human. By this recovery of consciousness as method, the theologian likewise moves to a perspective from which the conflicts within Christian theology and the conflicts posed by the diversity of other religious and non-religious ultimate value systems all become potentially intelligible. Through a methodical dialectic of the conversions, intellectual, moral, psychic and religious, which demand expansion of and even radical shifts in the theologian's own frontier of vision, he or she can come to appreciate and evaluate the embodied values of diverse traditions. To be in touch with the unfolding desire of the human spirit in its liberating imperatives, be attentive, be intelligent, be reasonable, be responsible, be in love, is to be lured to acknowledge all that is true, to love all that is of value. A therapy which facilitates the illumination of this eros serves to heal the human spirit at its profoundest level.

Chapter III
Religion As Spirituality: A Foundational Inquiry

This third chapter will delve more fully into specifically religious consciousness. As such it will be an exercise in foundational theology as Lonergan understands the term, "an objectification of conversion provides theology with its foundation."[1] The previous chapter was largely concerned with the categories of intentionality analysis which are common both to theology and to all other human pursuits. From the theological perspective Lonergan refers to them as general theological categories.[2] They are basically the four levels of consciousness and their structure, operation, articulation and dialectical development.[3] The special categories which are the focus of this present chapter on foundational theology are the articulation of religious conversion in terms of interiority analysis. They are special to the discipline of theology.[4] Like the general categories they too are cross-cultural at base. Their articulation obviously is not. The realities underlying the general and the special categories are the foundation of theology and clearly also the foundation for the meeting of religions. Those realities are ourselves.

This chapter then will be a foundational reflection on religion as spirituality. As such it will further develop the experiential basis of Lonergan's theological position and will advance the argument for a foundational theology along the lines Lonergan suggests. Included in this chapter will be Lonergan's grounding of religion in religious experience and the development of the categories with which he treats religion. A precise rendering of his understanding of religious experience begins the exploration into foundational theology.

Religious Experience

The term, religious experience, as Lonergan uses it, needs interpretation. Lonergan has located religion at the highest, the fourth level, of human self-awareness, the level of decision and love.[5] Experience, on the other hand, is his term for the most basic, the first level, of human awareness, the level of apprehension of data. On which level then is religious experience, the level of data or of love? In Lonergan's thought is *experience* which is *religious* a contradiction in terms? By no means. For beyond the meaning of experience as the level of attending to *data,* there is a broader meaning to experience in which it is identical with consciousness itself, with the *subject's presence to himself or herself* in each of his or her operations.[6] It is in this sense that a reference to religious experience in Lonergan's terminology is both intelligible and helpful. It refers to the *awareness* immanent in one's highest operation, one's fourth level performance, one's orientation to the Transcendent. Religious experience means personal consciousness of being drawn toward the ultimate.

A further clarification is also necessary. Lonergan does not wish to confine the term, religious experience, to religious existence that one is consciously adverting to. If religious experience is taken to mean the awareness immanent in one's religious consciousness, it must not be taken to deny that one can be living at the level of religious existence without attending to it.[7] Although it might at first seem strange to apply the word, religious *experience*, to a state of religious existence one is not aware of, it does not involve a contradiction. It is not even an unusual psychological occurrence. Frequently, for example, we operate out of feelings and even out of compulsions which we do not attend to but which may be quite obvious to others and which a skilled professional can help us acknowledge and name. One can have a feeling, e.g., anger or frustration, which one is only dimly aware of and not able to identify, but which dominates one's choices and actions. On coming to name the feeling, one will readily acknowledge that one was *conscious* of, one *experienced* this disturbance, but had yet no handle for it. Similarly, one can be acting out of feelings of deep love, whether of another or of the Ultimate, and yet not have attended to it or given it a name. After it is named, one can easily admit that one had experienced it without knowing what it was. Lonergan uses Maslow's terminology here. One can have peak experiences, here religious experiences, without attending to them. "Such experiences do not bear a label. When they occur, they are not accompanied by a small voice that assures you, you are having a peak experience."[8] One can have religious experience, then, namely living from the resources of abandonment to the Ultimate, without attending to it.

But I said Lonergan's use of the term, religious experience, is precise. Besides being conscious of oneself as religiously alive or operating religiously without attending to it one can express and objectify one's experience. One can move beyond religious experience to religious understanding and judgment. By religious experience Lonergan does not mean that further move, but a word must still be said about it. That move to expression and formulation is a spontaneous and natural one, and it has religious experience as its base, but religious experience is not that further step to expression, to understanding, and to judgment. "To say that this dynamic state is conscious is not to say that it is known. For consciousness is just experience, but knowledge is a compound of experience, understanding and judgment."[9] Religious experience is religious awareness; it is not yet and may never become full religious knowledge. Description of the religious experience and the development of categories from the description would first be necessary.

This relationship between consciousness and knowledge is not unique to the religious sphere. One can be conscious of oneself understanding or judging without formulating and constructing a cognitional theory. That is, one can be aware that one understands without going the further step of analyzing one's acts of understanding and forming judgments about it. Similarly, one can experience oneself living out of religious love, without analyzing the experience. One can attend to something without coming to full knowledge of it. But any level of human consciousness, the experiential, the intellectual, the rational, the decisional can also itself be the *object* of conscious experience. It can also be understood, judged, and action taken on it. For example, one can experience oneself understanding or judging or deciding and one can understand how one understands or judges or decides. One can use a first, second, third or fourth level operation on a first, second, third or fourth level performance.

In summary, religious experience for Lonergan is living at the stage of surrender to the Transcendent. It refers to that level either as explicitly and consciously attended to or as real and operative but not acknowledged. Further, religious experience can and does express itself. It is at the level of decision and action, therefore expression is connatural to it. As an operative state it can also be reflected on and rationally evaluated and so become knowledge, properly so called.

Lonergan's analysis of religious experience as well as his entire cognitional theory is meant to have general applicability and not to be confined to the Western and the Christian. The transcultural aspects of Lonergan's reflections, although alluded to earlier, require further consideration and are the focus of the next section.

Note on Transcultural Theory

Lonergan's cognitional theory is in intent cross-cultural, although, since developed out of the Western philosophical tradition, it is not so in its form.

> ... clearly it (transcendental method) is not transcultural inasmuch as it is explicitly formulated. But it is transcultural in the realities to which the formulation refers, for these realities are not the product of any culture but, on the contrary, the principles that produce cultures, preserve them, develop them. Moreover, since it is to these realities we refer when we speak of *homo sapiens* it follows that these realities are transcultural with respect to all truly human cultures.[10]

Lonergan's cognitional analysis is definitely cross-cultural *in intent* since it refers to cognitional processes common to all human knowing and choosing by whomever and in whatever culture. It is, however, not cross-cultural *in form* since surely even to raise the question, "What do I do when I know?" is to stand within a particular cultural tradition. To acknowledge this cultural context for the exposition is not to imply that the analysis is not true for those not in that tradition, but only that they might not easily or immediately consider it to be true, even if it were a perfectly accurate description of their own knowing. It is also not to imply that cross-cultural contact and further reflection would not serve to develop and nuance the cognitional theory.

The distinction between intent and form is of quite central importance to any enterprise such as Lonergan's, which endeavors to be cross-cultural, not only in its analysis of cognition, but in its analysis of religion and religious experience. The matter is further complicated when one enters into dialogue with other cultures and religious traditions which do treat in much detail the questions of knowledge and, more to our purpose in this study, religious experience. An alertness to the difference between trans-cultural intent and form will hopefully be obvious in the sections which follow.

General and Special Theological Categories

In addition, however, to matters which are in intent cross-cultural but in form perhaps not, there are matters peculiar to a particular culture or religious tradition. Careful distinction will have to be made between those elements in Lonergan's thought which are understood to be cross-cultural though the formulation is not cross-cultural, and those elements which are acknowledged to be Western and Christian. Lonergan himself does not always in his specific analyses make sufficiently obvious this distinction between an account of religious experience according to transcendental method and the terms — I refer especially to: love, gift, God — in which it is seen in the Christian tradition.[11] This is particularly so in the chapter "Religion" in *Method* and in some articles. The distinction is clearly made and its importance indicated, however, in the chapter "Foundations" under the headings "Categories," "General Theological Categories," and "Special Theological Categories."[12] It is pertinent but mostly only implicit in his other treatments of religious experience. It is clearly of key importance to the subject matter of this study since the heuristic character of Lonergan's work on religions is seriously impaired if his treatment of religious experience can only be interpreted in Christian terms.

Lonergan introduces the distinction between general and special categories in the context of indicating that the philosophical shift from metaphysics to cognitional theory has its implications for foundational theology.[13] Where previously, in Roman Catholic tradition, doctrines, e.g., grace, were interpreted according to metaphysical terms, the task now is to interpret them in terms of intentional (interiority) analysis, in terms of experience.

General theological categories are those derived from transcendental method. Their base is the human subject, attending, inquiring, reflecting, deliberating. As grounded in the cognitional and conative operations of the human person, their foundation is transcultural and their validity broadly based.[14] The sets of terms and relations which can be derived from interiority analysis are manifold. Among them: patterns of experience that are biological, aesthetic, intellectual, religious; patterns derived from the proper and full functioning of the various levels of consciousness and from their incomplete or distorted functioning; patterns of reflection and meaning appropriate to philosophy, theology, the natural and human sciences, and everyday experience.[15] From these terms and relations a systematic account of values, beliefs, meanings, and their dialectical development can be formulated. General theological categories are categories which are shared with other disciplines.

Special theological categories pertain to religious conversion and are proper to theology. Religious self-transcendence is an intentional state possible in any spiritual tradition and even outside of one. It is important to note specifically that for Lonergan, religious self-transcendence, the reality that Christians refer to as grace, is trans-cultural and, therefore, a subject for special theological categories. Individual traditions will have their own specific terms to refer to it but the reality is cross-cultural and this reality is the concern proper to theology. Religious self-transcendence is a reality prior to and deeper than any formulation of it.

> ... God's gift of his love (Rom. 5,5) has a trans-cultural aspect. ... if it is apprehended in as many different manners as there are different cultures, still the gift itself as distinct from its manifestations is transcultural. ... It is not restricted to any stage or section of human culture but rather

is the principle that introduces a dimension of other-worldliness into any culture.[16]

Lonergan's reasons for this affirmation of the trans-cultural character of religious self-transcendence are both historical and theological.[17] It is sufficient to note here merely that he considers it to be the reality at the base of special theological categories. The same general state can be spoken of in many different ways in different religious traditions. To describe that state, however, as "the gift of God's love" is to speak of it in specifically Christian terms. This is not to imply that special categories are necessarily simply equivalent across different traditions. It is, rather, only to delineate the task and suggest the possibility of establishing both the differences and the similarities on an intentional transcultural base.

The notion of special theological categories opens up the possibility of a new type of theology of religions which could *both* be based in a specific tradition and yet also be cross-cultural. The eventual foundation also for a *collaborative* theology of religions among the different religions themselves is possible on these terms.

Lonergan's understanding of special categories encourages the theologian to describe religious interiority initially in psychological terms, which can be seen to have general validity across religious boundaries, and then to speak of it in the terms of his own tradition.

> . . . because we acknowledge interiority as a distinct realm of meaning, we can begin with a description of religious experience, acknowledge a dynamic state of being in love without restrictions, and later identifying this state with the state of sanctifying grace.[18]

Special categories when presented in psychological terms are descriptions of religious interiority which have cross-cultural validity. They are further specified in different traditions. Special categories, which are finally those of interiority, are used as religious affirmations and not only as phenomenological descriptions, e.g., the doctrines on grace or the divinity of Christ. Often in the doctrine the phenomenological base in terms of the believer's experience is not readily apparent. The effort to unpack the phenomenological base is the work of interiority analysis. Lonergan's notion of special cross-cultural categories based on interiority analysis can help the adherent to a religious tradition locate within his experience what is referred to by his beliefs and can help him relate his religious experience to his other human experience. It can also provide a base and a heuristic for understanding others' religious experience as well as their beliefs.

The need for the development of a cross-cultural common language is clearly recognized by Raimundo Panikkar also:

> An interreligious dialogue worth the name has to begin by propounding a common language, meaningful to the different partners. Because religions are deeply rooted in the different historical traditions of the world, it is very difficult to find a terminology meaningful in more than one religious tradition. Secular present-day parlance, on the other hand, common as it is becoming, is branded too freshly by its marks of secularism and desacralization to make it acceptable to many of the people seriously concerned with religious values. This is indeed a difficulty, though perhaps our current and contemporary philosophical language may enable us today to reach a common ground, provided we keep it open and sensitive to the sphere of religion.[19]

At this stage of the meeting of religions such common language is still to be developed. Lonergan's work is a contribution to that enterprise. The following section presents certain of the basic "special" theological categories which Lonergan develops. They focus on religious interiority. Lonergan frequently does not clearly differentiate in his own writings between special categories which even now can be recognized as cross-cultural and specific Christian formulations of those categories. The following analysis will attempt such a differentiation on his principles. It will attempt to highlight the principal elements of his understanding of the state of religious self-transcendence. It is his view of the spirituality which is the base of religion and of post-critical theology. I have italicized for emphasis its key features.

Religious Interiority

Religious self-transcendence is *experienced* before it is, if ever, objectified and explicitly known.[20] It is a *call*, perhaps only dimly recognized, to *fearful* but *fascinating mystery*. It evokes both awe and terror.[21] It is a profound and dynamic *movement* toward an *unknown holiness*.[22] Its demands are *absolute*; it admits of no qualifications or reservations.[23] It calls for self-surrender, for response from one's whole heart, mind and strength.[24] One is *possessed* by it: it floods one's heart. It brings *fulfillment, joy* and *peace*.[25]

In the religions which speak of God, *it gives the divine name its primary and fundamental meaning*.[26] But *as an intentional experience*, which is not always either recognized or expressed, *it can be shared by those who believe and those who do not*.[27] It is Rudolf Otto's *mysterium fascinans et tremendum,* Paul Tillich's "ultimate concern," Ignatius Loyola's "consolation without cause" as Karl Rahner interprets it.[28] It is the experience of the mystic; negative theology is content to say what it is not.[29]

Thus, briefly, in terms of religious interiority, is Lonergan's description of religious experience, religious self-transcendence. What is attempted in Lonergan's description, as presented above, is an exposition in terms of interiority analysis using as little as possible the symbols and expressions proper to a particular religious tradition.

The language even of interiority analysis, however, is mostly derived from religious tradition and usage, although here used descriptively rather than normatively. This does raise possible conflicts with the way some traditions would speak of religious self-transcendence. The summary presentation in the first paragraph of this section attempted to be sensitive to this difficulty, particularly in not describing religious self-transcendence as love or the object of religious intentionality as the lovable. In many religious traditions, including the Bhakti traditions in Hinduism, Mahayana Buddhism, and, of course, Judaism and Christianity, such language raises no problems. Lonergan frequently uses the word, love, as a shorthand both for this transcendent state and for the object of the state. He clearly recognizes that love is not the universal description of religious transcendence and in fact even states that to some non-Christians it might be looked upon as a *specifically Christian* apprehension of the experience: "the adherents of non-Christian religions may wish to ascribe (to Christianity) the characterization of religious experience as being in love."[30] But certainly it is not an exclusively Christian characteristic.

The language of love is not necessary though to express religious interiority and, for the purposes of providing a heuristic description which can be recognized as possessing broad validity, such language is not helpful. Although Lonergan uses the word, love, in describing the reality of religious self-transcendence while writing for a largely Christian and Western audience, he recognizes that it need not be expressed in those terms. When religious interiority is not interpreted as a movement of and toward transcendent love, it can be experienced and interpreted as movement to transcendent mystery. "It is, then, an orientation to what is transcendent in lovableness and when that is unknown, it is orientation to transcendent mystery."[31] That this is a far from pejorative distinction will be clear from our later treatment of mysticism. As orientation to mystery, religious interiority awaits interpretation.[32]

Religious interiority is the crucial element, the basic and radical[33] element in Lonergan's understanding of religion and, hence, of religions. He calls this element by many names, some of which have already been introduced, but it is the same reality he is referring to by each of the terms: religious self-transcendence, religious experience, religious commitment, religious interiority, religious conversion.[34] Personal religious involvement is the peak state of conscious intentionality. Since Lonergan's philosophical and theological perspective is transcendental method — the conscious processes of our knowing and choosing common to all these operations — it is clear why the *conscious* state of religious *interiority* would be the key element in his interpretation of religion. It and the other elements drawn from intentionality analysis are his heuristic for understanding religion in all its manifestations.

The following description makes clear that this highest level of self-transcendence is the foundational element of his analysis of religion. Four other complementary elements necessary for a full account of religion — community, history, development, and breakdown — are interpreted as elements of the process of conversion, which is religious interiority.

> When conversion is viewed as an ongoing process, at once personal, communal and historical, it coincides with living religion. For religion is conversion in its preparation, in its occurrence, in its development, in its consequents, and also alas in its incompleteness, its failures, its breakdowns, its disintegration.[35]

Religious interiority establishes a context.

There is a further element pertinent to Lonergan's treatment of special theological categories which should be treated before turning to specifically Christian categories. It concerns religious consciousness as inexpressible. It is Lonergan's understanding of the mystic.

The Mystic

A consideration of the mystic should further serve to differentiate religious self-transcendence as an experienced intentional state, from special theological categories of a specific tradition. The mystic emphasizes the unknowing which characterizes his experience. He passes through or beyond the symbolic and meaning categories of his own tradition even if he then returns to them.

> Not only can one's prayer consist in letting lapse all images and thoughts so as to permit God's gift of his love to absorb one, but also those that pray in that exhausting fashion can cease to pray and think back on their praying. Then they objectify in images and concepts and words both what they have been doing and the God that has been their concern.[36]

The mystic withdraws from the world where reality is mediated by meaning, both everyday meaning and religious meaning, to a world of immediacy. When this takes place, "there is a withdrawal from objectification and a mediated return to immediacy in the mating of lovers and in the prayerful mystic's cloud of unknowing."[37] The world of religious immediacy resembles the infant child's world of immediacy. But here what is experienced directly is not the stimulated senses but one's own spirit drawn to and longing for the Ultimate. The Ultimate is mediated by the immediate experience of oneself moving toward the unknown. "When finally the mystic withdraws into the *ultima solitudo,* he drops the constructs of culture . . . to return to a new, mediated immediacy of his subjectivity reaching for God."[38]

The mystic's experience differs in degree but not in kind from the experience of anyone living at the level of religious interiority. For both there is the experience of interior immediacy, of inner movement toward the transcendent. There is at least a partial withdrawal from the world of history and meaning to experienced immediacy. The difference is in the stage of religious development, in the individual's temperament, and in the intensity of the experience.[39] The mystic possesses a highly differentiated religious consciousness.[40] The normal believer, although perhaps profoundly religious, is not so differentiated. With Lonergan's perspective of interiority analysis, it is clear why the mystic would be the paradigm of religious interiority. For the mystic's spiritual experience would be distinguishable from, even if not separable from, his or her other experiences.

Mystics are a phenomenon in all religious traditions: East and West, developed and primitive.[41] The highest manifestation of religious self-transcendence is found, then, in all the world's religions. The existence of mysticism, however diverse its various forms, is evidence that religious interiority, the special categories, has a transcultural base and manifestations.

The distinction between theistic and atheistic mysticism, e.g., Christian and Buddhist mysticism, Lonergan sees as possibly the difference between an experience which is expressed *and* objectified, theistic mysticism, and an experience which is left unformulated, atheistic mysticism. The Buddhist does not wish to withdraw from the mystic experience itself into affirmations about it.

> What is transcendent is no finite thing. Finally anything affirmed is thereby objectified, and any objectification is a withdrawal from the ultimate solitude of the mystical state. The alleged atheism of the Buddhist may be, perhaps, the expression of a non-objectified experience.[42]

Lonergan from his Christian perspective expects that the experience of mysticism can best be interpreted in personalistic terms. But a tradition of prayer and mysticism which stresses the movement to the unknown, the transcendent mystery, would deny or not attend to that element of the experience. Such mysticism remains genuine religious self-transcendence.[43]

It is well to point out here that Lonergan's theology of religions does not stand or fall on the basis of his specific judgments about elements of other religions. He is primarily a theological methodologist in his own work in this area, not a historian of religions or even a systematic theologian, except in so far as his methodology establishes a basis for the construction of systematic theologies. As he points out very strongly, the categories which a theologian elaborates and his evaluation of their truth and value — here the personal or non-personal understanding of mystic experience — depends on his intellectual, moral, religious and psychic development. There are no criteria which can rightfully be imposed; there are only the criteria which emerge in a subject striving for self-transcendence.

> The purification of the categories — the elimination of the inauthentic — is . . . effected in the measure that theologians attain authenticity through religious, moral, and intellectual conversion. Nor may one expect the discovery of some "objective" criterion or test or control. For that meaning of the "objective" is mere delusion. Genuine objectivity is the fruit of authentic subjectivity.[44]

Lonergan's own judgments on religious phenomena obviously depend both on the sources he uses for his information and also on the authenticity of his own religious and intellectual conversions. Lonergan's specific judgments and even his elaboration of method can be corrected then from within the horizon of the basic intentionality analysis which he espouses. A different evaluation of the relation of personalist and non-personalist mysticism is quite possible on the methodological grounds which Lonergan lays out. It is precisely the flexibility of Lonergan's method in matters such as this which makes it valuable and which serves to encourage both collaboration and continual revision.

We turn now to a treatment of the Christian special category of "grace." We choose this category because Lonergan devotes considerable attention to it in his recent writing and because it is the Christian interpretation of what has been presented as spiritual self-transcendence.

Grace

Having introduced the basic elements of Lonergan's intentionality analysis of religious experience, we move from these special categories to the specific formulation of these categories in the Christian religion. For the Christian, religious conversion is the gift of God's love. What leads to conversion and what sustains it is God's grace, and specifically God's grace received through Jesus Christ.

Lonergan seldom makes references to scripture in his later writings. In *Method in Theology* he gives as his reason that he is working as a methodologist concerned with operations rather than as a theologian concerned with objects.[45] Although he does not explicitly acknowledge it in *Method*, while acknowledging it elsewhere,[46] he writes of grace as a systematic theologian. In fact he specifically describes an intentionality analysis of grace as one of the tasks of systematic theology.[47] Accordingly, he invariably refers to scripture in his consideration of grace. Although he does not exegetically analyze the texts,[48] his own concerns appear from the texts he chooses. The frequency of his references to certain texts indicates their importance to him.

God's love floods our hearts through the Holy Spirit which is given to us (Rom. 5:5). There is nothing in life or death, or in any powers of the universe which can separate us from this love we experience in Jesus Christ (Rom. 8:35, 38-39). This love calls for response from our whole heart, soul, mind, and strength (Mk. 12:30; Deut. 6:4).[49] God himself is love (I John 4:8).[50] The gift of God and his love is to bear fruit in our lives (Mt. 7:16, 30).[51] It grounds our faith and makes it active (Gal. 5:6).[52] It manifests itself in kindness, goodness, fidelity, gentleness and self-control (Gal. 5:22).[53] Compared to the gift of love, everything else is useless (I Cor. 13).[54] There is an anonymity to this gift of the Spirit; it blows where it wills (John 3:8).[55]

In sum, God's love is a gift. It is unconditional. It calls for unconditioned response. This love transforms one's consciousness and manifests itself in one's actions. We receive this gift through Jesus Christ. The gift is God's own Spirit which brings alive whom he wills. These are the key elements in Lonergan's formulation of the Christian experience of grace. He understands it to be the same reality experienced, even if not so formulated, in all the religions of the world and also possibly by the atheist.[56] He takes this stand initially as a theological hypothesis and finds collaboration in the exposition by the historian of religion, Friedrich Heiler, of seven elements common to the major religions.[57]

Lonergan's analysis of self-transcendence has set the context in which this scriptural teaching can be understood. That context is the movement toward authenticity in human living.

> We have quoted Scripture but we also have provided a setting or context to elucidate the relation of scriptural doctrine to human living. We have found that to be authentically human is to transcend oneself, that self-transcendence raises the question of God, that the realization of self-transcendence occurs when we are in love, and that the all-embracing and deepest love is being in love with God.[58]

The human spirit in its development moves from the desire for truth to the desire for value. The desire for value is deepened and made stable through love: love of man and woman, love of friends, love of community, etc. But in addition to being in love with the finite, one can fall in love with the Infinite. It is that love of which the scripture speaks. It is a love which is unconditional and invites unconditional acceptance. It establishes a new base both for one's consciousness and for one's entire life. It is experienced as gift through Jesus Christ. The gift is God's own Spirit who goes where he wills.

Lonergan interprets this Christian teaching about grace in terms of interiority analysis. Lonergan had earlier analyzed grace in metaphysical terms in a series of articles, excerpts from his dissertation on *gratia operans* in Thomas Aquinas.[59] He does not wish to analyze it in those terms now. The intellectual horizon is no longer medieval. Metaphysics is not the basic discipline, but rather cognitional theory.[60] A critical metaphysics is derived from cognitional theory and epistemology. The contemporary theological task is to ground the specific categories of Christianity in the special categories of interiority analysis. The move to the subject has established a theological context that is no longer metaphysical but cognitional.

The analysis of grace has a very different constellation in a cognitional perspective than in a metaphysical one. The medieval teaching on grace presupposed a metaphysical analysis of the soul: its potencies, habits and acts. This was the order of nature. But grace is not due to nature; it perfects nature. Supernatural entities were called for which would be prolongations perfecting nature, although not derived from nature. These entities were habits and acts. The supernatural entitative habit rooted in the essence of the soul was principal or sanctifying grace. From it proceeded the supernatural operative habits residing in the soul's potencies. And from them proceeded individual supernatural acts.[61]

What is referred to as sanctifying grace in the metaphysical account is the dynamic state of being in love with God in the intentional account of self-transcendence. Neither the essence of the soul nor its faculties is data of consciousness. What is given in consciousness is the human subject, his various states, his intentional and performative operations, and the conscious linking of the operations or the states with one another. A cognitional analysis of grace is not, then, an analysis of metaphysical and non-experienced entities but of the conscious subject: his states, operations and their inter-connection.[62]

What is studied in the intentional account of grace is the process of conversion: its occasions, its conditions, its development, and its aberrations. Traditionally spiritual theology treated some of these matters in its discussion of purgative, the illuminative and the unitive ways.[63] In a cognitional analysis, spiritual theology, as a study of religious consciousness, takes center stage. Religious conversion is the principal subject matter of fundamental theology. Theology is challenged to keep close contact with living religion.

> But when conversion is the basis of the whole theology, when religious conversion is the event that gives the name, God, its primary and fundamental meaning, when systematic theology does not believe it can exhaust or even do justice to that meaning, not a little has been done to keep systematic theology in harmony with its religious origins and aims.[64]

Of course, the spiritual theology which can become the core of foundational theology is not the common sense compilation of spiritual maxims which some spiritual theology became. It attends to the dimension of subjectivity. It is post-critical. It takes the philosophical move to the subject seriously. Its simplicity is a tutored one. To use Ricoeur's provocative terms, the spiritual theology which is called for must be from the perspective of a post-critical second naivete, not of a pre-critical first naivete.[65] It must not prescind from the philosophical advance of the last three centuries, but must rather incorporate its gains and build on it. Not that spiritual conversion must be critically grounded to be genuine; religious conversion authenticates itself. But from the theological, i.e., reflective, perspective, however, it is only post-critical thought which clearly recognizes that the spiritual dimensions of subjectivity are the foundations of theology itself.

Having indicated the main lines of Lonergan's existential understanding of religion, our choice of the term "spirituality" to refer to it can perhaps be further developed now.

Spirituality

First, by way of contrast, it should be clear that by "spirituality" is not meant self-analysis or self-cultivation. That as a goal would be a form of truncated subjectivity. It would confine the human spirit. What is meant is that vista of human intentionality, that *transformation* of the self, which opens to what is beyond the self, the absolutely Transcendent. I use the word, spirituality, in addition to, and sometimes in preference to, religious conversion. Each highlights certain features of religious consciousness. Conversion emphasizes the *moment* of turning rather than the *state* of openness which results from the new vantage point, which spirituality expresses better. Both aspects are obviously essential. Spirituality also emphasizes the *continuity* with the whole unfolding intentionality of man's spirit: cognitional, moral and religious. It does not express as clearly as conversion, however, the necessity of the liberation from other drives, such as the tendency to narrowly focus on body, or ego, or self, which must be transcended if the human spirit is to reach beyond itself. In interreligious dialogue, spirituality has the advantage of already being an accepted term for the reality we are indicating.[66] Further, conversion, in an interreligious context, can easily be taken to mean movement from one religious tradition to another, rather than what is shared by religious traditions. It is clear how such a meaning would cloud any, particularly Western, attempt to foster dialogue. But since Eastern traditions, as well as Western, can by the "spiritual" mean the ethereal, the merely individual, the nonengaged, it is also a term not without its dangers. It should be clear, however, that this is decidedly not our meaning. It is at least as strongly not the view of Lonergan. Religious consciousness — spirituality or religious conversion — is a praxis, an engaged human state. "In Buddhist terminology, spirituality also possesses the Wisdom of Action."[67] It is the same decisional level as active moral response to value. It is engagement with the absolutely Transcendent, which liberates one to engage, to respond to, and to create and transform the world of finite value, the world of persons, society, civilization.

Lonergan's understanding of what is basic to religion then approximates what is called spirituality. It is surrender to the Transcendent, with the consequent transformation of subjectivity. What is foundational for religion, therefore, is also foundational for post-critical theology. Theology becomes reflection on lived religion. Christian, in particular Roman Catholic, theology has in its history placed religious doctrine at the base of theology and not religious existence. On the other hand, the Asian religions of Buddhism and Hinduism understand themselves as spiritualities rather than as doctrinal systems. If Lonergan is correct in his methodological probings, then it is both accurate and fruitful for the believer-theologian to understand spirituality as foundational for religion, including Christian theologians understanding Christian spirituality as basic to Christianity. Then the similar self-understanding in these three major traditions establishes a climate for the sharing of believers at the level of living religion and of the sharing of theologians at the level which is considered basic by all involved.

Summary

This chapter and the previous one have presented the two interconnected contributions to a Christian theology of religions that I wish to highlight in this study. The recovery of the interrelated operations of human subjectivity which was explored in the previous chapter provides the base for a theology which can integrate theory and praxis (the first three levels of consciousness and the fourth). It can, therefore, contribute to resolving the dichotomies which would isolate the religious and moral dimensions of the person and of societies for the apparently more objective pursuits of the sciences and technology. Such an approach to human subjectivity also takes seriously the turn to the subject which is such a major emphasis of modern philosophy. And it takes it seriously by effecting it and not merely discussing it. The therapeutic recovery of the subject as method is a personal act, or rather an open-ended series of personal acts in which one's own subjectivity effects the unveiling of one's own subjectivity.

Such subjectivity in its religious dimension was the theme of the present chapter. Its aim was to explore religious existence itself as decisional. Lonergan's understanding of religious experience was interpreted in that light. The dimension of religious interiority as self-surrender to the Transcendent was specifically presented. Its non-verbal quality was indicated in reflection on the mystic and the naming of that religious state as grace in the Christian tradition was pointed out. Finally, the aptness of the term, spirituality, to refer to the transformation of the self in religious surrender was considered. All of these elements served to focus on the praxis which is central to religion, what Lonergan calls "falling in love with God."

With spirituality as religiously foundational and interiority therapy as intellectually foundational, the theologian who would understand his own faith today and who would dialogue with other faiths is on firm ground. For dialogue and self-understanding both call for one's own resources to become increasingly transparent and both spiritual conversion and interiority therapy facilitate such transparency.

The following chapter will raise significant and related further questions pertinent to a deepening and development of a Christian theology of religion. The theologian will be considered as psyche, an understanding of Christianity will be explored, and the relationship between theology and the history of religions will be analyzed.

Chapter IV
Further Questions: Psyche, Christianity And The History Of Religions

A host of further questions present themselves whenever a subject as broad as the one investigated in this study is pursued. I have chosen to focus on three areas which expand the inquiry one step further in different directions. The first section will present reflections on the pyschic dimensions of religion and of the theologian. It will specifically consider the structure of Christian redemption. Human subjectivity has been at the center of the entire work. A consideration of psyche and the cross will broaden the concern with subjectivity. The second section will be a textual inquiry into Lonergan's understanding of the distinctiveness of Christianity. It should facilitate the fuller self-understanding of the Christian theologian who would adopt the perspective of interiority analysis. The third will be a consideration of the relationship between the history of religions and theology, or more precisely, between the history of religions and the theologian. It will reflect on the special questions pertinent to each and to the interrelationship between the questions. Foundational theology is not an isolated discipline and an analysis of the connection between the history of religions and theology will indicate how it can be enriched by the science of religion and what theology's role is, consequent to the findings of that science.

Psyche, the Intentional Task and the Cross

Lonergan's intentionality therapy leads to the reflective recovery of the subject. He or she is the foundational reality for theology. The full recovery of the foundational subject, however, demands more than the *cognitional* or even the religious dimensions which I have so far emphasized. A cognitional recovery of itself would certainly demand the shift of theological foundations from affirmations to the horizon of the subject who makes them. But the critical mediation of meaning through cognitional therapy does not reveal the whole subject. Lonergan is clear on this point although he does not develop it: ". . . there is the mediation of immediacy by meaning when one objectifies *cognitional* process in transcendental method and when one discovers, identifies, accepts one's submerged *feelings* in psycho-therapy."[1] Psyche, the world of affect and symbol, is integral to human subjectivity. Its recovery, in addition to the recovery of the intentional and of the religious subject, is necessary for a foundational theology which is liberated not only from myths about knowing but from the tyranny of disordered affect, of domination by injurious archetypal imagination. Scheler's *Ressentiment*[2] and Neumann's *The Great Mother*[3] convincingly demonstrate the crippling of the subject when affect and symbol are not brought into the light of consciousness and integrated into the personality. The particular importance of psychic conversion[4] for religious consciousness and hence for foundational theology is twofold. First, religious consciousness as orientation of the subject to the Ultimate, i.e., as moving beyond itself to the Other, intends every other level of self-transcendence which can foster and support this final self-forgetfulness. Therefore psychic healing is intended in religious consciousness so that religious consciousness can move toward full term. Secondly, religious consciousness expresses itself most adequately in the limit language of symbol and myth, whose wellspring is the psyche. If symbols, archetypal and personal, and their concomitant affects are misperceived and distorted by the subject, then the Transcendent intentionality of religious symbol will likewise be misperceived and distorted, and the fuller development of spiritual conversion will be truncated.

The articulation of the full intentionality of the human person demands, then, psychic conversion. The recovery of the subjectivity of the religious person involves a negotiation of the images and feelings which are characteristic of the religious level. Surely one knows without naming the cognitional moments of human intentionality, so one responds to the Ultimate and chooses values over satisfactions without articulating the elements characteristic of spiritual and moral subjectivity. But if the task is that of foundational theology today, especially foundational theology in dialogue and dialectic with other religions then one is challenged to bring to consciousness the full structure of authenticity. That includes a recovery of psyche in her imaginal and affective dimensions.

The foundation of theology is then in the limit the fully converted subject. Converted subjectivity is led to by symbolic limit language and in turn expresses itself most adequately in imaginal terms. The foundation of theology is not, however, confined to one's own converted spirit. One's own conversion opens up for one the horizon of spiritual conversion wherever it is discovered. It is not limited then even to one's own faith community. To so limit it, when the effects of conversion are abundantly evidenced outside one's tradition is to act arbitrarily, i.e., through a failure in conversion. As a consequence, a full foundational theology must dialectically examine and appreciate the images, the limit symbols, not only of one's own tradition but of other traditions. This is so, not in the first place to provide a foundational theology for all religions, though that is its direction, but to provide an adequate and articulated foundation for one's own limit language.

In other words, if the structure of human subjectivity is accurately even if incompletely presented in Lonergan's analysis of the unfolding of consciousness and if the imaginal is the vehicle of religious consciousness, then a dialectical, aesthetic analysis of the principal archetypal symbols of the major religious traditions is necessary to understand the broader and universal significance of one's own tradition. The analysis must be aesthetic since it involves symbolic imagination. It must be dialectical since religious, moral and psychic criteria must be applied to the analysis. The delicacy and precariousness of these analytic operations needs again to be highlighted. The analysis is done by the theologian-believer. The presence or absence, or probably more to the point, the degree of his/her aesthetic, religious, psychic, moral and intellectual conversion is directly pertinent to the limit of competence with which the analysis will be done. Just as one's own conversion is directly pertinent to one's ability to evaluate the analysis. There are not criteria which can be used apart from those understood and accepted by the subject-theologian-believer. But one is not trapped by this subjectivity. As has been emphasized repeatedly, subjectivity is self-transcending and counter-positions invite their own reversal.

The task, then, of evaluating the archetypal, cross-cultural religious symbols is fraught with difficulty. An example might clarify. Robert Doran has pointed out how even that most sensitive guide to cross-cultural images, Carl Jung, through a probable failure of religious intentionality, takes the view that there is good and evil in God rather than the view that acknowledges His transcendent goodness.[5] Jung expounds his view in "Answer to Job."[6] "To believe that God is the Summum Bonum is impossible for a reflecting consciousness."[7] Doran's evaluation, with which I am in agreement, is that Jung does not adequately recognize a distinction between ego-transcendence, namely, the movement into the deeper psychic resources of the self, and self-transcendence, the movement of the self to encounter the other, God and other people. The various forms of self-transcendence are collapsed into ego-transcendence.

Doran[8] finds a symbolic indication of Jung's failure to fully acknowledge the transcendence of the Divine Other in Jung's dream at the time of his composing "Answer to Job."

> At the top of the stairs was a small door, and my father said, "Now I will lead you into the highest presence." Then he knelt down and touched his forehead to the floor. I imitated him, likewise kneeling, with great emotion. For some reason I could not bring my forehead quite down to the floor — there was perhaps a millimeter to spare. But at least I had made the gesture.[9]

Jung's "millimeter to spare" is no doubt the difference between full submission to the Other and a refusal to do so at that point in Jung's life. The simulation of submission is not adequate. Not to finally acknowledge the Other could have prevented Jung from making the distinction between the finite characteristics of the human self, namely, good and evil, and the quality of God's transcendent goodness. It is that full goodness of the Divine which alone frees man to face both sin and the whole interior journey through darkness with confidence both of forgiveness and of healing. Jung's view is an inflation of the self. Submission in the dream would have been recognition of the difference between creature and creator and adoration, the appropriate expression.

My point in raising this example is not primarily to affirm that Doran's analysis is accurate, though I do think it is a plausible hypothesis, but to indicate precisely the delicacy of such an evaluation despite its interest and its value. Jung interprets the story of Job in the light of his own dream. Doran evaluates both Jung's interpretation and Jung's dream. I agree with his evaluation. You, the reader, evaluate all of us. The levels of conversion of the traditions to which we belong and our own personal conversion — intellectual, moral, religious, psychic, aesthetic — within those traditions are obviously pertinent and operative in our evaluation. To evaluate is to take a stand. And a stand to what one is personally responsible for. It depends on one's own development, on the flowering of one's own intentionality.

Yet to take a religious stand is to affirm not only that it is valuable but that it is true. It demands for its full truth claim an analysis of alternative images and formulations as well as their evaluation. A religious stance today entails a claim to universality. The age of the tribal god is gone. The early vedic period and the early hebrew period are not options. One is led, then, particularly one who would articulate foundational theology, to an understanding and evaluation of men and women's cross-cultural religious experience and expression. Again, the point is that such an evaluation is called for to ground adequately even a particular tradition. It is indeed then also a service to a theology of religion, not religions, as a long range goal. But immediately it serves to locate and explain the saving message for the sake of the believer's own affirmation. He or she has a need to situate the experience and expression of his/her spirituality in order to take it with full seriousness.

The work of Sebastian Moore, particularly his seminal study,

The Crucified Jesus is no Stranger,[10] deserves treatment in regard to our reflections on the cross-cultural investigation of the psyche. Like Lonergan,[11] he focuses on the cross as the central Christian mystery. He goes into a more precisely detailed psychological analysis, however, about the actual process of transformation of evil into good which occurs in the human heart as it is face-to-face with the Crucified. The categories which emerge from psychic conversion provide the terms for explicitating the process of spiritual conversion. In Sebastian Moore's study, psychological categories also illuminate the distinctive characteristics of conversion within the Christian tradition. They suggest a base within the foundational event itself, which is religious conversion, both for the communality of spiritual transformation which is shared across religious traditions and for the specific features of Christian conversion. I consider Sebastian Moore's treatment because it is a striking and significant example of theology after the model espoused by Lonergan and considered in this study. It takes seriously the shift to religious subjectivity as foundational for theology. And it gives evidence of the fruitfulness of this horizon both for the Christian community itself and as a Christian contribution to the dialogue of religions. It interprets the specifically Christian message of redemption in terms intelligible on a transcultural psychological base. In Lonergan's terms, it interprets the specific categories of Christian redemption in psychically grounded special theological categories. The terms of the central Christian mystery of the redemption are interpreted, not in explanatory metaphysical terms, but in the explanatory terms of psychological interiority.

Two points which are central to Moore's exposition of the process of redemption are first, his use of psychological concepts and second, his precise understanding of the notion of sin. Sebastian Moore uses categories developed by the analytic tradition of Carl Jung, in particular the concepts "ego" and "self." The "ego" is man's conscious personality. The "self" is the complexus of powerful non-conscious resources within the human person. There is a decisive difference, however, between Moore and the Jungian tradition on the status of the "self" and on the process of coming to terms with the "self." It is the difference between staying within the workings of the psyche and, instead, recognizing the intentionality of the psyche, the matter of engagement with the Other. That engagement indeed is imaged in the relationship of "ego" and "self" but its end is beyond it. The psychologically reductionist tendency which is present in some of Jung's disciples is pointedly expressed by Edward Edinger. "In fact when the Christian myth is examined carefully in the light of analytical psychology, the conclusion is inescapable that the underlying meaning of Christianity is the quest for individuation."[12] Religion serves the psyche; the cross of Christ serves individuation. Rather, in Moore's view, religion illuminates the *plight* of the psyche and heals it by effecting the move beyond it; the cross of Christ makes explicit man's sin and effects thereby man's reconciliation with God. "The crucified . . . transforms evil into sin into grace . . . evil made totally explicit is resolved in the forgiveness of God."[13]

How Moore understands this religious transformation in Christianity will become clear. That Moore by the use of psychological concepts, especially Jungian ones, does not fall into the trap of psychologism must be clear from the beginning. Beyond the transcendence of the ego into the self, there is the further transcendence of the ego and the self into encounter with the Divine.

The Jungian error is subtle but disastrous. The "self" as the locus of the *indefinite* resources of the human psyche is the most powerful personal image of the *Infinite*. With this Moore agrees. The "self," however, is not the Infinite. With this Jung[14] and Jungians[15] agree. The Jungian tradition, in fact, issues stern warnings about the inflation which not infrequently occurs when the resources of the self come into consciousness. One can consider oneself to be God or at least try to act as such; one can act out the Icarus myth. At this point, however, Jungians, such as Edinger, succumb to inflation themselves. They become so fascinated by the God image of the "self" and by the process of coming to psychic wholeness — the "ego" coming to terms with the "self" — that they effectively interpret that very process to be salvation. The intentionality of the "self" beyond the "self," particularly in terms of the Absolutely beyond the "self" is truncated. Sebastian Moore's analysis, on the other hand, is not only post-critical — it formulates from the perspective of religious and cognitional subjectivity — but it is also post-therapeutic — it articulates the intentionality of the psyche beyond itself.[16]

We turn now to Sebastian Moore's analysis of sin. It is central to his exposition and it illuminates not only the problem of redemption but the similarly basic Christian affirmation of the goodness of God. In concert with Lonergan's own analysis of evil, it clarifies this recurrent and central problem, which appears in all religions, of the relationship of the Transcendent to evil.

The key to understanding the precise character of the evil of sin is to understand in what sense it is *unreal* and yet has *devastating reality* in its consequences. It is the choice of vacuum rather than value and that vacuum destroys. Moore affirms that sin has "no being. The only kind of 'being' it can have is the sight of itself in its ultimate effect, the crucified."[17] This view corresponds precisely with Lonergan's understanding of "basic sin " and the consequent moral evil that follows from it: ". . . basic sin is not an event . . . it consists of a failure of occurrence in the absence in the will of a reasonable response to an obligatory motive."[18] Yet "what could and ought to be but is not"[19] has a powerful effect: "by moral evils I shall mean the consequence of basic sins."[20] How is this possible? Basic sin is a failure of self-transcendence, a failure to respond to value at the responsible level of intentionality. "It is the inescapable narcissism of our consciousness."[21] And that narcissism, that absence of self-transcendence which could and which ought to have been achieved has real and powerful negative consequences. Not only does the self-making which is the creative effect of responding to one's moral intentionality to the good not happen, but from this absence there follows "moral evils of omission and a heightening of the temptation in oneself or others to further basic sins. From the basic sin of not setting aside illicit proposals, there follows their execution and a more positive heightening of tension and temptation in oneself or in one's social milieu."[22] The refusal of Jesus' crucifiers of the religious self-transcendence to which they were challenged effected the crucifixion. To comprehend him they would have had to transcend themselves and they did not. The evil of basic sin wreaks havoc wherever it occurs.[23]

The careful understanding of sin as *irrational*[24] *absence* and yet having *power* in its effects significantly illuminates two persistent theological problems: the seeming inadequacy of defining evil as the privation or absence of good, given its palpable reality, and the challenge to the goodness of God if evil exists. For if there is evil, God must ultimately be the cause of it and therefore God is not good. Both Moore and Lonergan hold that the devastating effects of sin exist but they are precisely the effects of what *ought to have existed* and yet by irrational decision *does not*. To understand basic sin then is to understand it precisely as a *privatio boni*, that is its ultimate evil. A good does not exist which man's intentionality demanded. To consider basic sin as privation is not then to disregard evil but to locate precisely *how* a sinful choice is evil. The non-existence of the self-transcendence which might have been is the basic evil. Privation of the good is the name of that evil. The type of evil which involves non-existence needs no cause for *what is not* cannot have a cause. And "if basic sin cannot have a cause, God cannot be this cause . . . Besides the actual good that God wills and the unrealized good that God does not will, there are the basic sins that he neither wills nor does not will but forbids."[25] God's goodness is not *directly* challenged by the existence of sin. But the *indirect* challenge remains. Why does God create a universe in which the possibility of sin obtains? And even if God is not the cause of sin because of its unreality, still the evil physical and psychological consequences of basic sin exist. In a world of emergent probability and freedom, however, they need not be considered ultimately and unmitigatingly evil. They do not negate the goodness of God. Lonergan's own careful analysis of the goodness of God and the problem of sin and moral evil deserves quotation in full:

> Clearly, it is not evil but good to create a being so excellent that it possesses rational self-consciousness whence freedom naturally follows. It is not evil but good to leave that freedom intact, to command good indeed and to forbid evil, but to refrain from an interference that would reduce freedom to an illusory appearance. Consequently, it is not evil but good to conceive and choose and effect a world order, even though basic sins will and do occur; for it is only fallacy to argue that basic sins either are entities or nonentities and that, if they are entities, they must be due to God's universal causality, or if they are non-entities, they must be due to God's unwillingness

to cause the opposite entities.

There remain physical and moral evils. Now if the criterion of good and evil are sensitive pleasure and pain, then clearly physical and moral evils are ultimately evil. But the proper criterion of the good is intelligibility, and in this universe everything but basic sin can be understood and so is good. For the imperfection of the lower is the potentiality for the higher; the undeveloped is for the developed; and even moral evils through the dialectical tension they generate head either to their own elimination or to a reinforcement of the moral good.[26]

God's goodness then is not inconsistent with a universe in which the good of freedom demands the possibility of sin and in which the evil consequences of sin can be overturned. The responsibility of sin rests squarely on man. Lonergan's dialectical analysis of good and evil which corresponds to Moore's understanding of sin makes problematic any view that the Transcendent is beyond good and evil in the sense that the evil in the world demands that evil be included in God. This hits again at the Jungian view[27] that confuses the image of God which is the psyche and which includes good and evil with the One who transcends the psyche. Because there is evil in the one does not mean there is evil in the Other.

Although I have chosen Jung as the example of an opposing view of God, the distinctions Lonergan and Moore make could be helpful in interreligious dialogue, particularly in the dialectical moment. A failure to confine evil to man and the location of it as well in the Transcendent can lead to the failure to acknowledge the distinctions between the Transcendent and the human, and it can also lead to distortions of morality in the name of the Transcendent.

In Sebastian Moore's study of human evil and the Crucified, he searches for the "linch pin,"[28] the intelligibility, of the relationship between Jesus and his crucifiers and the intelligibility likewise of the transformation which occurs in the believer who allows the challenge of Jesus crucified into his heart. In the crucifixion the believer is faced with the irrational act, the basic sin, of Jesus' crucifiers. Their unintelligible refusal to transcend themselves results in the destruction of the Innocent One. In the objective destruction of Jesus, the believer is confronted with what is his own basic sin, his own destructive rejection of the "fullness of life . . .

which our own being dreads. Some unbearable personhood, identity, freedom, whose demands beat on our comfortable anonymity and choice of death. Further, something that at root we *are*, a self that is ours yet persistently ignored in favor of the readily satisfiable needs of the ego."[29] In the crucifixion, we see lived out in history[30] the drama which each of us engages in, the destruction of our own self-transcendence, of the intentionality of our "selves," by our ego's persistent choice of its own "egoistic self-importance."[31] "The art of contemplating Jesus crucified is to come to understand . . . that the cross that I always first experience as 'life's crucifixion of me' is in reality my crucifixion of life, in other words the Jesus-cross."[32] In the historically crucified, the believer then is faced with the self-crucifixion which his own narrow ego inflicts on the resources of life, resources with which he might have created not only himself but a world with others to the praise of God. The death of Jesus makes explicit the persistent death man inflicts both on himself and on others. And the very explicitness of the sin entails not its victory but its transformation. Three particularly illuminating passages from Moore develop this theme.

> The ultimate truth, which is God's unique embrace, is that the essential effect of sin — the crucified — is, identically, the healing. What sin ultimately *is*, is seen in the crucified. What sin ultimately *is*, is forgiven. For sin brought to its ultimate succumbs to God's love. It cannot be otherwise. It suffices for God to make our elusive evil explicit in crucifixion, for it to be no more.[33]
>
> What I have, in the sight of Jesus on the cross, is not the *motive* for believing in God's love so that this belief will *then* overcome my self-hatred, but the actual *process*, made visible, dramatized in the flesh, whereby my self-hatred reaches its climax of realization, avowal, confession and surrender. Man's self-hatred is not only the *obstacle* to his acceptance of God's love. It is the *medium* in which God's love is revealed to him as it transforms it. I meet God's love not by turning away from the hatred of myself to another motif, but as a climax of my self-hatred, its crisis and resolution. God does not just give me *reason* not to hate myself. He transforms my self-hatred into love. That is the meaning of the cross.[34]
>
> This is the ultimate mystery of us: that even our evil, even

our tendency against wholeness, exposes us to the love of God. And it exposes us to that love in a way and at a depth to which even our desire for wholeness does not expose us. Jung insists that evil has to enter into our integration and charges Christianity with leaving it out. Jung is right about evil. It has to enter. In an unfathomable way it *desires* its own transformation. But evil enters into the total transformation only through crucifying Jesus.[35]

Evil becomes the *felix culpa* not only of Adam's sin[36] but of the sin of Jesus' crucifiers and of our own sin. Through the process of coming to terms with it we are redeemed. Moore analyzes the transformation of "evil into sin and sin into grace"[37] with the categories of interiority which are developed by Jung. Moore first asks, "who *are* we, that we are *thus* lost, *thus* rediscover ourselves, and are *then* recovered by an all encompassing love?"[38] He responds that "it is hardly to be doubted that the answer has to be on the lines of a distinction between the ego and the self. Generically . . . evil consists in an infinite variety of alienation between the conscious ego of man and a total self in which he has his place in God's world. And so generically, salvation consists in the overcoming of protean alienation."[39] But Moore issues a caution about dealing with the self. When one does gain access to some of the resources of the self, there is a strong temptation for the ego to appropriate the gain for its own aims. That aim can involve a self-fascination through which the ego uses the depths of the quest for human totality to replace the proper living out of the human "in its context of history and society."[40] He insists that the dialectic between ego and self, between crucifier and crucified, is never finally resolved in this life, "as long as I live in this world, my life will move — in rhythm with all the complexities of being a participant in the mystery of evil and its redemption — between the poles of crucifier and crucified."[41] That bracing fact that my redemption is not a final achievement in this life undercuts the pretensions of the ego and in so doing actually facilitates the redemptive process. It is in the death and rising of Jesus that redemption is objectively achieved. And it is face to face with the crucified that it is appropriated in one's own life.

Moore's analysis takes with full seriousness the imagined and psychic dimension of religious conversion. And he does this in terms of psychological categories which have recognizable cross-cultural meaning. This is of service both to interreligious dialogue and to Christian self-understanding. Moore's study is firmly within the horizon of intentionality analysis and is derived from his own experience as believer, theologian and spiritual director.[42] Moore does not consider his work final and it is not. Other attempts must be made to name the process which is Christian conversion. If there are many theologies in the New Testament, one should not expect fewer now. But this is to take nothing from Moore's theology of redemption. It can stand on its own as a penetrating study of the psychic structure of salvation in Christ. And for the purposes of this study it indicates with a concrete instance the fruitfulness of the project which was proposed in the first three chapters.

The following section will detail Lonergan's method at work on a task correlative to that of the present section. It will focus on the specific structure of Christianity. Picking up themes of intentionality analysis and of spirituality considered earlier, it will further consider them in relationship to the distinctiveness of Christianity.

The Distinctiveness of Christianity

This section has two functions. The first is methodological: to see Lonergan's mind at work theologically, to see his method in operation. There is this caution however. Although Lonergan addresses himself to the distinctiveness of Christianity on a number of occasions in recent writing, he does not give it a detailed or systematic treatment. One cannot judge it then as a complete theology of the question. We will bring together recurrent features of three of his treatments of the matter to establish his position in its basic outline. Our results will then be *indicative* of the direction of his thought. During and after the period of the development of *Method in Theology* he only infrequently directed himself to a specific theological question.[43] The uniqueness of Christianity is one of those questions. Since Lonergan insists that the discovery of intellectual method is consequent upon intellectual performance, it is quite in keeping with his analysis of understanding to study method in operation: ". . . in human affairs there are some things which are understood before they are done, and others which must be done before they can be understood; and all intellectual activity is of this latter type."[44]

The second function of this inquiry into the distinctiveness of Christianity pertains even more directly to the purpose of our entire study. For the dialogue of religions, Christianity must articulate its own self-understanding. It is important to discover the self-understanding which arises from Lonergan's viewpoint. Although that understanding is until the present only expressed in articles rather than a full length study, still what is gleaned does shed light on the question.

The purpose of this section then is twofold: to discover the content of Lonergan's position on the distinctiveness of Christianity and to uncover elements of his theological method.

It is wise, as the results and methods of redaction criticism indicate, to presume that no statement of an author is merely casual. Evidence for a statement's insignificance should be brought forward rather than proof needed for the contrary. If this is a wise presumption with regard to any writer, it is doubly wise with regard to Lonergan. Anyone at all familiar with Lonergan's writing realizes how far from casual is any statement of his. The presumption that each of his remarks is significant will be operative, therefore, in this study as it has been throughout, and will demand on occasion a detailed analysis of his statements.

Lonergan treats of the distinctiveness of Christianity and the correlative question, its similarity to other world religions, in three writings in 1969-1970: "The Future of Christianity,"[45] "Faith and Beliefs,"[46] and "The Response of the Jesuit, as Priest and Apostle, in the Modern World."[47] In each of these he treats of the elements common to all religions and the features distinctive of Christianity. He does not discuss the distinctive characteristics of the other world religions but acknowledges such specific elements and indicates they must be attended to.[48] Both in the articles and especially in an address in 1975, he indicates that that attention should be given in the context of interreligious dialogue.[49]

Considering each of the three articles in turn will permit us to establish both the content and the context of Lonergan's discussion of the identity of Christianity. Recurrent features in his analyses will bring into relief the principal elements of his position and of his method. And attention to individual statements will serve to qualify and expand these elements.

"The Future of Christianity"

Lonergan at the start establishes a working meaning for what is meant by *religion*. He ". . . will draw attention away from what is outward and toward what is inner and vital to religion."[50] This is consistent with the position articulated earlier in the study on the centrality of spiritual conversion. He achieves this delineation of what is inner and vital by summarizing the seven elements of Friedrich Heiler's account, from a history of religions perspective, of the areas of unity of the world's religions. There is transcendent reality. That reality is immanent in human hearts. It is for man, the highest good, supreme beauty, truth and righteousness. That reality is ultimately love, mercy and compassion. The way to that reality is repentance, purification, prayer. That way is also love of one's neighbor and even of one's enemies. The way most supremely is love of the Transcendent, union or dissolution into it.[51]

With this as a base, Lonergan poses two questions: the first, leading to an analysis of the intentional structure of the human subject and the second, posing a question from a Christian theological perspective: "First, what is the function of religion in human living? Secondly, how may a Christian account for the great similarity in the diverse high religions without denying the uniqueness of Christianity?"[52]

The function of religion. The first question is answered by a succinct presentation of his analysis of the four levels of consciousness, the stages in self-transcendence. Religion is the ultimate horizon. The other levels of consciousness pertain to lesser perspectives. Religion exists on the highest level of self-transcendence, the level where the individual *abandons solitude*. He or she falls in love. In religion, that love is love of God. In referring to this love of God, Lonergan quotes his favorite passage from Paul, "Through the Holy Spirit given to us, God's love has flooded our hearts" (Rom. 5:5).[53]

The uniqueness of Christianity. Having indicated the principal element in religion and having located it on the highest level of human development, Lonergan proceeds to pose the problem of the uniqueness of Christianity. The distinctiveness of Christianity is not in the *possession* of God's grace but in the *mediation* of God's grace. "What distinguishes the Christian, then, is not God's grace, which he shares with others, but the mediation of God's grace through Jesus Christ our Lord."[54] It is not, then, in the achievement of self-transcendence that Christianity is distinctive but in *how* that self-transcendence is achieved. Sebastian Moore's theology of the cross, as we have seen, is an explanation of precisely the *how*. It is not Christian teaching that living on the highest level of self-transcendence is limited to Christians, although, using the term grace or gift of God's love to refer to that reality is a Christian theological expression. On the empirical level the existence of spiritual self-transcendence in other than Christian contexts is borne out by Heiler's account of the common features of the world's religions.

The other, the "outer" features of Christianity — doctrine, history, social forms — derive their specific characteristics from Christ, the mode and medium through which Christians achieve self-transcendence.[55] For in addition to the internal gift of God's love which is the inner core of all religiousness, there is the specific, historical, interpretive word who is Jesus Christ.[56] Christians witness to an event: the cross and resurrection of Jesus.

Lonergan then develops the features of Christian community — features *qua* community common to any religious community, features *qua* Christian having their own unique embodiment. The interior word of God's love is not an isolated or isolating word. ". . . the gift of God's love, however personal and intimate, is not so private as to be solitary. It is given to many through Jesus Christ that they may be one in him."[57] God's love binds together those who receive it. Those who receive it need one another to understand the inner and outer word of God to them. Since personal transformation is slow and precarious, Christians need the support and encouragement of one another. Teaching, preaching, ritual and common worship bind Christians together, allow them to share what is deepest to them, and provide encouragement and challenge to those who fail.[58] All of these features, except for the specifically Christian outer word of the life, death and rising of Jesus flow from the common characteristics of community: the human need for intersubjectivity, the developmental aspects as well as the precariousness of self-transcendence.

Already it is clear that Lonergan's interpretation of the communality of Christianity with other religious traditions and his interpretation of Christian uniqueness center on elements which have their place in cross-cultural general and special theological categories. They have meaning in terms of interiority. There is the self-transcendence of religious conversion. There are the elements common to communities. There is progress, decline, and the need for redemption both in individuals and in communities.[59] The interpretation of the meaning of the Christian outer word of the death and resurrection of Jesus is developed elsewhere by Lonergan.[60]

Lonergan has indicated that Christian community is historical both in its element of witness to an event and because the inner word likewise demands community over time. Now for any group or movement to endure through history it must adapt to various cultures. If it is to accomplish this and still retain its identity it must make what Georg Simmel called *die Wendung zur Idee*, the shift to the idea; it must understand its own core meaning. This shift to the idea denotes

> . . . the tendency and even the necessity of every large social, cultural, or religious movement, to reflect on itself, to define its goals, to scrutinize the means it employs or might employ, to keep in mind its origins, its past achievements, its failures.[61]

There follows a brief analysis and history of the major cultural transpositions in Christianity, especially in Roman Catholicism. He develops particularly the transition from what he calls classicist culture to modern culture.[62] Classicist culture understood itself normatively and abstractly. Modern culture understands itself both empirically and concretely. It acknowledges variation, development and breakdown. It studies each of the many cultures of mankind. It seeks to understand all of the features of the cultures, especially those which classicist cultures would dismiss as strange or barbaric.

> Instead of thinking of man in terms of a nature common to all men whether awake or asleep, geniuses or morons, saints

or sinners, it attends to men in their concrete living. If it can discern common and invariant structures in human operations, it refuses to take flight from the particular to the universal, and it endeavors to meet the challenge of knowing people in all their diversity and mutability.[63]

Where before man sought to understand the objective universe and then himself in terms of it, now man first seeks to understand himself. He realizes that it is through his own eyes that he will grasp the universe. Cosmology is replaced by anthropology. And with that transposition follows a transposition in religion and in theology. Man and his horizon takes precedence over *what* he knows. Religious self-transcendence then becomes the context for understanding one's beliefs. "An existential approach reveals that fundamental differences do not lie in this or that particular doctrine but rather in one's personal stance and one's resulting outlook. It seems to follow that if we take our stand on the common stance and outlook produced within and beyond the Christian communion by God's gift of this love, there is bound to arise and to be sustained an efficacious desire for sincere and, may it please God, fruitful dialogue."[64] On the common base of self-transcendence the diversity and the uniqueness of the various revelations will become manifest. The outer word of Christianity in Jesus will be understood from the perspective of the inner word. And from the perspective of the inner word which is shared in the various religions the outer word of Jesus and the other outer words can be perceived and understood.[65] The cultural shift to historical consciousness along with the concomitant shift to intentionality analysis establishes the perspective from which Christianity and especially in Lonergan's case, Roman Catholicism can dialogue with other traditions.

In summary, religious self-actualization is a common feature of the world's religions. Christians call that self-actualization grace, the gift of God's love. The uniqueness of Christianity is the medium through which that grace is experienced. Christianity has existed in many cultural forms. The present transition to historical-mindedness provides the perspective from which dialogue among the various religions can be effectively pursued.

We turn now to a second article, "Faith and Beliefs," in which the uniqueness of Christianity again is considered.

"Faith and Beliefs"

Lonergan begins by referring to a lecture by Wilfred Cantwell Smith in which the symbols used in religion are distinguished from the basic religious attitude expressed through and even beyond the symbols. Both the symbols and the attitude revealed through them are to be attended to.

> To live religiously is not merely to live in the presence of certain symbols but, he urged, it is to be involved with them or through them in a quite special way — a way that may lead far beyond the symbols, that may demand the totality of a person's response, and may affect his relation not only to the symbols but to everything else: to himself, to his neighbor, and to the stars.[66]

These symbols, following Smith, Lonergan will refer to as "belief" and the basic religious attitude he will call "faith."[67] This faith is what is common to all religions; it is universalist.

> So conceived, I think, faith would not be the prerogative of some particular church or religion. It would not be merely ecumenical but universalist. It would be relevant to an understanding of any and every religion. Moreover, its relevance would be of the highest order, for unless one understands what personal involvement in religion is, one can hardly be expected to think or speak very intelligently of religiously committed persons.[68]

As a Catholic theologian Lonergan acknowledges that before Vatican II such a universal view of faith would have been unacceptable to Catholics; now it is an obligation for Catholics to think this matter through. The remainder of "Faith and Beliefs" is such an attempt.

Four questions are posed to which a note of special significance to our investigation is added after the answers are presented:

> First, what is man's capacity for religious involvement? Secondly, in what precisely does this religious involvement consist? Thirdly, in what sense can such an involvement be called faith? Fourthly, what is the relation between such faith and religious beliefs?[69]

There is also a preliminary qualification made before Lonergan proceeds. The empirical evidence needed to support his responses to the four questions cannot be provided nor even expected in such a brief essay. His answers, therefore, should be considered as aids to understanding which might be of some assistance when the occasion arises for one to describe reality.[70]

Man's capacity for religious involvement. Lonergan presents a rather full account of the four levels of self-transcendence. He calls special attention to the fact, however, that the spatial metaphor of levels is precisely a metaphor and introduces the notion of sublation from Rahner to lead the reader beyond imagination. The relation of each new sublating set to the previous sublated set is one of retention, extension and completion.[71] Our capacity for religious involvement lies in our capacity to live on the highest level of self-transcendence.

What is religious involvement? Having indicated our capacity for faith, Lonergan describes the achievement, the actual living on the fourth level of self-actualization. All love is on the highest level. The love of God is the fullest achievement of love; it is being-in-love in an unrestricted manner. The experience of that love is the experience of mystery. In Christian belief it is called the gift of God's love. It is not an exclusively Christian phenomenon, however, for its characteristics, as Heiler describes them are common to all the world's religions.[72] In fact, it is most likely present in even less developed forms of religion.

> There is then a line of reasoning that suggests that a basic component of religious involvement is the same in the world religions. But may one not extend this view to the more elemental forms of religion? Can one not discern in them the harvest of the Spirit that is love, joy, peace, kindness, goodness, fidelity, gentleness, and self-control (Gal. 5:22)? As a theologian holding that God gives all men sufficient grace for salvation, I must expect an affirmative answer; but as a mere theologian, I must leave the factual answer to students of the history of religions.[73]

Lonergan recognizes a clear distinction of roles between the theologian and the historian of religions. We will explore this distinction further in the third section of this chapter. Here we merely note the distinction of function and Lonergan's desire as a theologian to remove restrictions on where the fullness of self-transcendence may be discovered.

Religious involvement and faith. If religious involvement is basically faith, then love seems to precede knowledge. Yet, *nihil amatum nisi praecognitum.*[74] It is true that knowledge generally precedes love but this is not so with the love of God. Love in this instance provides the perspective, the principle for further, fuller knowledge. "It is a knowledge of values and disvalues, of good and evil. It is a knowledge that consists in one's response to the values and disvalues and, more specifically, in the development, strength, fulness, refinement of one's responding."[75] The knowledge that love gives, that self-transcendence gives is "the reasons of the heart," of which Pascal speaks.[76] The connection among religious and moral and even intellectual conversion is implied here. Spiritual self-transcendence reveals both spiritual and moral values and in our own time the realization of both demands the intellectual asceticism which is involved in overcoming common myths about knowing. Faith, universalist faith, is the transformation of one's values that comes from loving God in an unrestricted way. This transformation of values is a religious constant; the specific values transformed may vary, the process does not.[77]

Religious beliefs. Religion is an affair of the heart but it is not a solitary affair. It can be shared by many and finds expression in the total fabric of our lives. The experience of loving God in mystery can manifest itself, objectify itself in any cultural period or context. Hierophanies and the Gods of the world religions are all manifestations of the same basic process of our reaching to express the transcendent. They are also manifestations of our failure to express the transcendent because of our failure to attain or sustain self-transcendence.[87] This process of expression is both individual and communal. We largely receive rather than personally constitute the world of religious meaning, of beliefs, in which we live.[79]

Use of the model. Having answered the four questions posed at the start, Lonergan adds a final section which is of special significance for the content and method involved in the question of the distinctiveness of Christianity. Lonergan again reiterates that he has intended to provide in this essay only a general construct, to work out in broad terms the distinction between a faith which proceeds from the love of God in self-transcendence and the various beliefs, acts of meaning, in which that faith is expressed and developed. As a model it does not intend to account for any specific set of beliefs.[80]

To be concrete, the analysis Lonergan presents not only does not seem to account for but even seems to run counter to Catholic Christianity. His position seems to be an acceptable modernist one but can it be the position of a Catholic theologian? The specific point which would be offensive to Catholics in Lonergan's construct is the position that belief is merely the objectification of religious experience. Catholics hold that their beliefs, especially the events of their founding, are special acts of God in history, the word of God expressed.[81]

To counter this difficulty and to explain what modification the model must receive to be pertinent to Catholicism, Lonergan uses the analogy of human love. He suggest that this is the experience operative in the belief that God speaks in human terms. Just as the love of a man for a woman would be truncated if it were never expressed, so too one might imagine that the love of us for God and God for us would be deficient if not only we but also God did not express his love in a special way.[82] The principal occasions, therefore, when we came to self-transcendence in the Judaeo-Christian tradition are interpreted to be at the same time occasions when God by a special act intervened in human history.[83] The modification of Lonergan's model, then, to account for Catholicism is not to alter the position on the universality of faith but to understand the process operative in the Catholic faith perspective which leads it to interpret certain historical events as the externally uttered word of God.

In brief, we find reiterated again in this article that religion is the achievement of living on the fourth level of self-actualization; that religious living, now called faith, is a recurrent feature in all of the world's religions, including the elemental; that faith expresses itself in multifaceted and diverse beliefs; and that Christianity has certain specific belief characteristics. These specific characteristics center on the belief that God actively intervenes in history, especially in the events of salvation. These special features in Christianity can be understood on the model of the need for human love to express itself.

We now turn briefly to a third consideration by Lonergan of the characteristics of Christianity.

"The Response of the Jesuit"

At a first glance in a surprising context, an address to Jesuits, one finds an analysis of Christianity and the other world religions. I say at first sight such a strange context since the previous two articles were directed to obviously broad topics and one would expect the focus here to be narrower. From another perspective, however, when one realizes that in the earlier essays Lonergan was speaking not from outside but from within his own faith context — the context of a Christian, Catholic, Jesuit, theologian — in addressing the question of Christianity and world religions, it is not surprising that when he speaks to his own context he brings to it the reflections which originally had risen from it.

The article has six headings. All but one of these parallel what we have seen above: that one, *Sending*, on apostolic ministry in the early church is not immediately pertinent to our study. Since repetition at this point is hardly necessary, a detailed presentation of the article will not be given. The six sections will be briefly summarized. Under *Authenticity*,[84] an analysis of the four levels of self-transcendence, especially the fourth is outlined. Human authenticity, self-transcendence, is presented as the achievement of the natural unfolding of human development. Under *Spirit*,[85] transcendence is described as being in love with God; the love of God is linked with the experience of mystery.[86] Under *The Word*,[87] the distinctive faith perspective of Christianity as well as a succinct characterization of world religions is indicated. We will return to this. Under *Sending*,[88] the early formation of the Church is considered. Under *The Renaissance Jesuit*,[89] and *The Jesuit Today*,[90] the transition from classical to historical-mindedness is presented and the constants and variables of Christianity are indicated. We will return also to this.

Content and Method

It would not seem presumptuous to assume that having examined in greater or lesser detail three studies which treat of world religions and Christianity we have available the outline of Lonergan's position on the uniqueness of Christianity. We have likewise attended to the key features of his method. We might summarize the content and lead into an explicitation of method by analyzing two succinct presentations on the nature of world religions, from *The Word* and on the special characteristics of Christianity from *The Renaissance Jesuit*.

So I am inclined to interpret the religions of mankind, in their positive moment, as the fruit of the gift of the Spirit, though diversified by the many degrees of social and cultural development, and distorted by man's infidelity to the self-transcendence to which he aspires.[91]

The three characteristics Lonergan singles out present what we have discovered about world religions in these articles. First, the world religions are described in terms of intentional analysis; not in the content of their beliefs but through the general structure of the human subject. Use of "gift of the Spirit" indicates that the summary is from a Christian theological perspective but it is none the less an intentional analysis for that. We have seen "grace" as the Christian equivalent of the affirmation that a person lives on the highest level of self-actualization. The second and third characteristics are developments of the first: that this self-transcendence expresses and hence diversifies itself in many cultures — we are still in the terms of intentional analysis since culture is a matter of constituted meaning — and that the achievement of self-transcendence is never total or lasting.

If these are the characteristics of world religions, what is specific about Christianity?

There are the constants of Christianity and the variables. The constants are man's capacity and need for self-transcendence, the Spirit of God flooding men's hearts with God's love, the efficacy of those that mediate the word of God by word and example, by linguistic and incarnate meaning, for *cor ad cor loquitur*. But there are also the variables. Early Christianity had to transpose from its Palestinian origins to the Greco-Roman world. The thirteenth century . . .[92]

The variables are themselves, in a way, a constant. The variables are the cultures through which Christianity has expressed itself. No one culture is necessary, but some culture always is. This is the first intentional characteristic. Our need for self-transcendence is a second, and corresponds to the precariousness of self-transcendence mentioned above. The third characteristic is the Spirit of God flooding our hearts with God's love; in other words, men and women living in authenticity and self-transcendence. So far the characteristics are merely consistent with the general analysis of world religions. He then specifies, however, what is distinctive about Christianity: its linguistic and incarnate meaning. This agrees with the previous discussion in "Faith and Beliefs" on what is unique in Christianity. It is not on the level of faith but on the level of belief that Christianity is distinctive.

Throughout the treatment of the question of the uniqueness of Christianity, the intentional structure presented with fullness in both *Insight* and *Method* is clearly the perspective which is operative in every aspect of Lonergan's consideration. The refusal to take imagination for knowing and religious conversion for intellectual conversion allows Lonergan to bring new insight into the Christian belief of God's intervention in human history. Likewise, intentional analysis saves him from the pitfall of attending first and chiefly to the content of the beliefs of the world religions, which stand in apparent opposition to one another, and permits him to focus on the structures and processes, which he considers to be basically the same.

In many ways, Lonergan's treatment of world religions and the distinctiveness of Christianity is a particularly transparent use of his method. Since in the form which the question exists today, the previous doctrinal tradition, except on grace, has little to say about it, Lonergan was in a particularly free position to develop theology in his own mode, without constant reinterpretation of the tradition. The richness and consistency of his method, therefore, stand highlighted in his treatment of the uniqueness of Christianity.

We turn now to our third further question, the relationship of the type of foundational theology we have developed in this study to the discipline of history of religions. That discipline in conjunction with dialogue among religious believers are two major sources for foundational theology along the line Lonergan suggests. They would also be major sources not only for Christian theology but for a common theology of religions such as Wilfred Cantwell Smith calls for.

The traditional form of Western scholarship in the study of other men's religion was that of an impersonal presentation of an "it." The first great innovation in recent times has been the personalization of the faiths observed, so one finds a discussion of a "they." Presently the observer becomes personally involved, so that the situation is one of a "we" talking about a "they." The next step is a dialogue, where "we" talk to "you." If there is listening and mutuality, this may become that "we" talk *with* "you." The culmination of this progress is when "we all" are talking *with* each other about "us."[93]

The History of Religions and Theology

The relationship between history of religions and theology is often problematic.[94] For the theologian, coming to terms with the history of religions is not only an instance of the difficult task of situating empirical studies in relation to faith, but it is especially the difficulty of integrating a discipline which appears to challenge, even if only implicitly, any exclusivist claims of one's own and of any particular faith. The problem for the theologian is further exacerbated by the reductionist tendencies of some of the schools of the sciences used in the history of religions, e.g., psychology, history and sociology. The theologian, then, is wary of the entrance of an apparently alien and threatening body of knowledge. The historian of religion, on the other hand, is frequently not interested in correlating a scientific and "objective" discipline with the obvious "subjectivity" of theology.[95] The theological question is also not immediately or clearly relevant to the historian's work.

I have located the problematic status of the relationship between the history of religions and theology in the practitioners of the two disciplines, for disciplines cannot cooperate, only people can. What impedes a working correlation between the two disciplines is that too few persons have been interested in the sets of questions asked by each, and thus have been unable to formulate the questions which would lead an individual from one to the other and back again. The history of religions has been for some an alternative to theology and theology has frequently not experienced the need for, or has been fearful of, history of religions.

There are surely sets of questions proper to each.[96] And those questions of fact and of value are not on the face of it, incompatible. When we have a stand-offishness of these two disciplines it is frequently because the horizon of faith is unable to cope with the horizon of modern scientific and historical consciousness, and the horizon of modern consciousness is indifferent to or lacking in comprehension of the horizon of faith. A general merging of horizons is still only dawning. Lonergan's work offers much to one who would attempt such a merger. So does the work of Joachim Wach and Wilfred Cantwell Smith. In the following reflections I will rely on each of them. In the first case, we have a theologian open to the history of religions. In the second, we have historians of religion open to theology.

To write of a merging or fusing of horizons on the part of the theologian and the historian of religion is not to advocate a drawing back from the hard-won separation and distinction of disciplines. That would be all loss and yet the same person can (and should?) ask both sets of question and hence can discover how they do indeed correlate with one another. Only chaos would result from confusing the sets of questions proper to each discipline.

The Horizon of History of Religions

The dispute — mostly resolved now — about what to call the scientific study of religions, "comparative religion" or "history of religions,"[97] highlights a significant facet of the perspective operating in the discipline. The scientific discipline which has developed is by strict intent descriptive and not evaluative. Typologies are indeed employed to relate the various constellations of characteristics of one religion to another — organizational, cultic, doctrinal patterns, etc. — and in that sense comparison is used. But comparison here is a method which serves for greater clarity of description and is not intended to be value laden. "Is this religion more hierarchically organized than this other?" "Does cultic practice play a more significant role in this religion than that?" The questions do not imply that a religion should be more rather than less cultic, that highly structured hierarchy is preferable to less structured. These questions are not denied; they are simply not asked in the discipline.

The questions which are operative in the scientific study of religion are "What is . . .?" questions,[98] rather than "Where do I stand with regard to what is?" or "Does this conform to the basic religious insight of . . .?" questions.[99] "What is?" questions do not demand on the part of the inquirer adherence to a religion. And in fact if the inquirer did adhere to a religion he or she would have to prescind from — not deny — the value judgments of that religion in his or her descriptive work.[100] "What is?" questions do not imply the invalidity of further questions, nor do the further religious questions imply the invalidity or uselessness of "What is?" questions. In fact the further religious questions presuppose answers to the "What is?" questions for the integrity of their own answers.

The historians of religion are "modern persons." The sets of questions which they ask have only become precise through the development of the various sciences. Their techniques are shared with or borrowed from other scientific disciplines.[101] What is unique to them is that data they deal with and the perspective from which they deal with it. As to their attitude toward the data, an openness toward the validity of religion would seem a prerequisite for understanding the uniqueness of the data involved. But in itself, the horizon necessary to engage in the history of religions does not logically demand that the historian have come to grips with questions of the type mentioned earlier: "Where do I stand personally with regard to what I have uncovered?" The impetus to the faith question, the theological question, does not derive from the demands of the discipline of history of religions but comes to the historian as a person faced with the necessity of taking a stand with his or her life.

In summary, the history of religions is an integral discipline in its own right. There is a horizon of questions proper to it. That horizon is available to modern historical and scientific consciousness. That horizon does not logically demand or presuppose a religious or faith horizon on the part of the historian of religion. A failure to have an empathy for the religious horizon, however, can block insight into the unique data being dealt with.

The Horizon of Theology

If the horizon of the historian of religion methodologically prescinds from faith commitment, the horizon of the theologian is founded upon it. It is not founded solely on it, however.[102] The theologian's faith stance, though, does establish both the primary reality that he reflects on and the context — the community — within which he reflects. The historians of religion depend on modern scientific and historical consciousness for their horizon; the theologians did not have to wait for this intellectual breakthrough to ply their trade, though today they ignore it at the peril of irrelevance. Lonergan's work and the burden of this study has been to explore precisely the contours of a theology founded on that shift to historical consciousness. But theologians can and most frequently operated from other intellectual horizons. The faith stance is the recurrent feature. The theologians' horizon is established intrinsically by their religious commitment itself and by the shared symbols and values of the community of which they are a part and upon which they reflect.[103]

Even such a preliminary contrast of horizons points out a built-in tension between the historian of religion and the theologian. For the historians of religion do not need a faith commitment for their work and theologians do not depend, in principle, on modern scientific consciousness for theirs. And yet theologians as persons in the twentieth century must come to terms with historical consciousness both for the integrity of their personal development as well as to communicate to individuals of historical consciousness, and the historians of religion needs to adopt a stance toward faith not for the sake of their discipline but for their own sake. The questions raised by the history of religion call for answers which historians of religion can dodge only at the price of their own authenticity. The tension between historians of religion and theologians does not come, then, from their having adopted *incompatible* horizons, but only from their limiting themselves to their own horizons.

Another source of tension is the particularity of theologians. It is true, as this whole study has tried to indicate, that simply by their religious horizon the theologian shares an analogous perspective with all believers in any religion. For they and all believers are functioning as such not at the level of intellectual or moral or aesthetic consciousness, but at the plane of radical openness to the Ultimate which characterizes religious consciousness. But religious consciousness is always embodied, always concrete. Theologians are opened to it through the images, symbols, teachings of those to whom they are exposed, and they do their own reflection and express their own faith in concrete symbols. They do not create the symbols of his faith nor can they alter them alone or at will. They both receive their faith and express it in a community.[104] Theologians' symbols are always the particular ones of their community — even when they are expanding the horizon and enriching the symbols of the community. The historian of religion's field of vision, on the other hand, includes in principle all the particular religious symbols of every community. Theologians must integrate and adopt affectively and personally the symbols that they employ. Historians of religion do not integrate and adopt all of the symbols they analyze and examine. They cannot and their work does not call for it. They need not resolve multiplicity, they must only accurately describe it. With this understanding the apparent confinement of the theologian, in contrast to the openness of the historian, can be appreciated. For the theologian's task is to integrate and not only to analyze.

Perhaps an example will clarify this difficult matter further. It is one thing to know the general structure of language and of particular language, another to speak many languages and even more to speak a language combining all the languages that one knows. The historian of religion must know the general structure of religion (language) and of a number of particular religions (languages); he or she need not as historian engage in any one religion (language) or still less create a new religion (language). The theologian as such need not know the general structure of religion (language) or of more than one particular religion (language), but as a person he or she must practice a religion (language).

It might help to pursue our language analogy a bit further to avoid the possible implication that there are absolute and *a priori* boundaries between languages (religions). History bears out that there is no such thing. New languages do emerge from the commerce of people. Indeed, new religions arise and religions in proximity to one another experience the influence of one another. There are no *a priori* limits on how languages or religions might change. There are, however, the present actual states and the past actual states of different religions which the historian of religions describes and analyzes. And there is the present actual horizon of the religion the theologian belongs to, however much he or she may be intending or succeeding in broadening it. One must not lose sight of either element, the actual or the potential in a religion.

It is beyond the human capacity of the theologian to achieve in himself the lived integration of all religions. Even if one world religion were a possible or even ideal goal, it would also be the work of centuries and of generations of believers. This clearly does not mean that the theologian should not take the lead in opening the horizon of his religion to the religious values of other faiths. Indeed, he should and must. But he cannot do the impossible. He must enrich his own community and not isolate himself from it by moving completely out of their religious horizon.

The historian of religion is under no such burden of personal synthesis, simply as historian. Faced with taking up a life-stance toward religion, the historian would encounter in this dimension of his or her life the same particularizing and enrichment as the theologian. And it would indeed be enrichment. For there is an arbitrary and unnatural confinement in limiting oneself to "What is?" questions and not asking the further "Where do I stand?" questions. Asking both sets of questions does not mean confusing them. Each set pertains to a different horizon. But there is every reason for a person to exist on both planes since both correspond to genuine human capacities and aspirations.

If the historian of religion is enriched by asking value questions, so is the theologian enriched by asking descriptive religious questions. That he has not in fact often let himself be so enriched is a lamentable aspect of much of even current theology.

In summary, the theological horizon is quite as valid as the horizon of the historian of religion. The one is essentially grounded in a faith-stance, the other must prescind from such a stance. The historian of religion has done his work when he has arrived at accurate description and understanding. The theologian, on the other hand, must take a position on what he has understood about religion and reflect on the nature and consequences of his stand and of the stand of the community in which he takes it. The development of the history of religions is not necessary for constituting the horizon of the theologian. Its methods and results, however, can enrich the theological horizon by providing the broadest possible base for the theologian's own decisions and by illuminating the elements of religion. Historically the theologian often has been reluctant to accept that broader base and the historian of religion has often shied away from the particularity consequent upon taking a faith stance. The breadth afforded by the history of religions has yet to be adequately received by theology.

The Horizon of Dialectics

We have pinpointed the basic experience which grounds theology as "taking a faith-stance," being converted. It is the "spirituality" which we have named as the core of religion. If the historian of religion does not have that experience, he cannot operate on the horizon of theology. We have also described what would principally accrue to both the theologian and the historian of religion if he were also able to function on the other horizon. Something more needs to be said, however, about the evaluative horizon which can mediate between theology and the history of religions. Lonergan refers to this level as "dialectics." It partakes of some of the qualities of each but can rightly be called a separate horizon. It is more than descriptive but it is still preparatory to adopting a faith stance or operating in one. It does involve a comparing and contrasting of religions, not for descriptive purposes but as evaluation. Its questions are "What are the weaknesses and strengths of individual religions?", "What is at the core of religions?", "What elements are simply cultural particularizations and not incompatible features of different religions?" These questions are more than merely descriptive. They provide the intelligent mediating step between the descriptive history of religions and the normative theology.

The horizon of dialectics is a little developed one and yet an obviously crucial one if the horizons of the theologian and of the historian of religion are to be merged and the riches of one pass to the other. The historian needs to evaluate before he can commit himself. But how is he to do that evaluation without asking some such questions? The theologian must likewise evaluate and compare the different religions if he is to let them alter and enrich rather than confuse his own theological horizon.

The frequent dichotomy between the faith horizon and historical consciousness has prevented the adequate development of this horizon of dialectics, yet it is precisely this horizon which can mediate between the other two. The historian is reluctant to evaluate lest he appear to compromise the objectivity of his descriptive work. The theologian is reluctant to compare his religion with other religions lest he seem to relativize his own faith position.

The development of this dialectical discipline does not become the less necessary, however, because it becomes the more difficult. Its necessity comes not primarily because of the existence of a lacuna between two disciplines but from the more basic human drive to ask all relevant questions. Its necessity comes from the logic of the mind's own inquiry. "What is it?" "What is significant about it?" "Where will I stand toward it?" The development of this discipline will help to fulfill this human and scientific gap. It will likewise save the theologian and the historian from the compromise they rightly seek to avoid. Lonergan has done significant work to flesh out this new discipline, to open up the new horizon.

A specific point of exegesis of Lonergan might serve to further clarify the discipline of dialectics. Lonergan indicates that religious conversion is not necessary to engage in dialectics or in the three prior specialties of research, interpretation and history.[105] But he means that in a very precise sense. He does not mean that it is indifferent whether one is converted or not. What he says is that conversion "does not constitute an explicit, established, universally recognized criterion of proper procedure in these specialties."[106] Lonergan chooses his words carefully. Conversion is not part of the "procedure" in doing research or writing history, even the history of religions. It is certainly not "explicitly" and "universally" acknowledged as a "criterion" in those disciplines. The religiously indifferent write history as well as the religiously committed. And of course commitment to a religion does not by itself imply the full meaning of self-transcendence which is Lonergan's understanding of conversion. And non-commitment to specific beliefs does not mean the absence of such religious self-transcendence. One cannot deny the name history to what an historian whom one considers to be unconverted has written. However, for Lonergan, conversion, as we have shown earlier, means the long process of overcoming of one's biases: intellectual, moral, psychic and religious; and to be unconverted means to be operating out of one's biases, and most probably out of unacknowledged biases. To be unconverted does not mean that one's procedures are unsophisticated but that one's ability to acknowledge the data, to interpret it with understanding, and to evaluate it accurately can be sorely askew. These are not irrelevant dimensions to the value of a work. Lonergan is simply then acknowledging facts when he says, "anyone can do research, write history, line up opposed positions."[107] His own words acknowledge some place for conversion, but he seems to downplay it: "when conversion is present and operative, its operation is implicit: it can have its occasion in interpretation, in doing history, in the confrontation of dialectic."[108] I would interpret his remark about conversion having "its occasion" as having two purposes. One is simply to recognize that history is indeed written from all imaginable perspectives. It has its occasion but it also has its non-occasion. The second is that in the later disciplines of dialectics and foundations biased perspectives from history can in principle be exposed and rooted out. In other words, there is a discipline which is capable of evaluating history and which attempts to overcome the effects of biases or distorted viewpoints. The evaluative perspective in dialectics is one precisely based on the criteria of the conversions; religious, psychic, moral, intellectual.

Anyone who can write the following about conversion and about horizons, which the conversions or the lack of them open or close us to, cannot be indifferent to the presence or absence of conversion in those who do history of religions or the history of Christianity.

> Conversion, as lived, affects all of a man's conscious and intentional operations. It directs his gaze, pervades his imagination, releases the symbols that penetrate to the depths of his psyche. It enriches his understanding, guides his judgments, reinforces his decisions.[109]

... horizons may be opposed dialectically. What for one is found intelligible, in another is unintelligible. What for one is true, for another is false. What for one is good, for another is evil.[110]

Horizons then are the sweep of our interests and of our knowledge; they are the fertile source of further knowledge and care; but they also are the boundaries that limit our capacities for assimilating more than we have already attained ... What does not fit will not be noticed or, if forced to our attention, it will seem irrelevant or unimportant.[111]

The historian whose eyes are not open to what is can hardly accurately present or interpret it in his or her writings.

But if I understand why Lonergan in the interest at least of common usage indicates that historians in their work need not be converted, I would take exception to his statement that conversion is also not necessary, though doubtless helpful, in dialectics. "Anyone can ... line up opposed positions." Yes, anyone can, but if the procedure is not to be a method which can be performed by rote, and particularly if the procedure of dialectics is to line up positions on the basis of the intellectual, moral, religious and psychic conversions involved, those same conversions to some degree would seem to be prerequisite for performing the task at all adequately. Admittedly dialectics as dialectics does not actually make choices among the horizons but simply exposes them. Still, without the conversions as a personal horizon, I fail to see how the dialectician can even accurately expose the positions. This point of the necessity of conversion in dialectics is important since unlike history which is an established discipline, dialectics is not established and it would be well in encouraging its development to indicate the irreplaceable necessity of the conversions for performing it properly. One's horizon is important, and the more explicitly this can be acknowledged and the broader the values one is sensitive to, the more significant will be the work and the more liberating it will be for others.

Dialectics and Dialogue

Beyond dialectics there is dialogue. Dialectics is the analysis and evaluation of the past, of others' actions and postures, in the light of one's own values. One must evaluate if one is to clarify one's own values in relation to the wisdom and foolishness which is one's own inheritance. But the emphasis in dialectics is best placed, I would suggest, not on critique of the past but on valuing the past. Dialectics is e-*valuating*, it is *co*-valuating, letting the values of the past reveal themselves and in the process letting one's own values come to light. Dialectics is best understood then as dialogue. One's own development is never complete. If the past stands in need of critique, which it does, so do you and I stand in need of critique. The humility which the fact of our own incompleteness, if not also our own willfulness, should engender is a dialogic rather than a dialectic stance toward the past. In dialogue, one can expect to be challenged by the values one had not yet discovered or perhaps had even uncritically rejected. This is to be as much an expected part of the process of evaluating the past as the discovery that in the past certain values had been dismissed or not yet uncovered. ". . . the very people that investigate the dialectic of history also are part of that dialectic and even in their investigating represent its contradictions. To their work too the dialectic is to be applied."[112] And the dialectic which is healing is called dialogue. "While the dialectic of history coldly relates our conflicts, dialogue adds the principle that prompts us to cure them."[113] The disposition to dialogue is a precondition for an accurate and empathetic appreciation of the other's values and affirmations. But the disposition to dialogue is not only a precondition for the understanding of the other, it is also the same disposition which allows one to grow in appreciation of one's own tradition and in the personal appropriating of that tradition. The disposition to dialogue is a value stance — as is also, obviously, the disposition not to dialogue — but the receptivity involved in a dialogical being-in-the-world indicates a growth posture. It acknowledges one's own historicity as well as that of one's partner and affirms not only that the past can be understood but that the future can be created out of the interchange.

In summary, dialectics is an evaluative discipline necessary both for the historian of religion and the theologian to mediate between their horizons. It needs a development comparable to the development in each of these disciplines since it too asks a significant set of human questions. It need not compromise either discipline since a merging of horizons does not mean a confusion about what question is being asked in what context but is simply the development of the latent ability to ask questions which are consequent upon one another. The authenticity of the person who attempts dialectics is even more important than the authenticity of those engaged in research, hermeneutics and history. Dialectics come to full term will be dialogue not only with the past but with present exponents of different traditions. And the disposition to such dialogue will itself be the type of personal and communal achievement that will have already moved one beyond the past. We have come full circle to the attitude expressed by Wilfred Cantwell Smith as quoted in the conclusion of our previous section: "The culmination of this progress (of dialogue) is when 'we all' are talking *with* each other about 'us'. "[14]

Conclusion

The human subject, individual and social, intentional and religious, has been the theme of this study. This chapter has considered three areas — psyche, Christianity, and the history of religions — areas directly pertinent to both the intentional recovery of the subject and the consequent grounding of foundational theology in a reflection on religion as spiritual conversion. The exploration of psyche touched on the further reaches of subjectivity and with the assistance of Sebastian Moore we investigated a possible structure of Christian conversion. A presentation of Lonergan's understanding of the uniqueness of Christianity followed. The inner reality of spiritual self-transcendence was seen as common to the world religions. The outer word of the life, death and rising of Jesus gives Christianity its distinctiveness. The history of religions and theology were next explored. The questions pertinent to each were identified and the horizon of dialectics was seen as mediating between them. All three areas of the chapter were presented to advance a foundational theology which would be sensitive to the Western turn to the subject and to the dimensions of spirituality which are central to Christianity and to the Eastern religious traditions. They pertain to the self-understanding, the theology, of one who would reflect today on who he or she is as a Christian and hopefully they also contribute to the communal self-understanding of all persons engaged in the spiritual quest. As reaching out to others, however, these considerations move beyond understanding to a disposition to dialogue and to cooperate. They pertain, even if only inchoately, to religious and intentional praxis.

The concluding chapter will present a final overview of the foundational concerns of this study and will indicate areas that call for further exploration.

Chapter V
Conclusion: Retrospect And Prospect

We live in a community of immediacy and of meaning, of a world we touch and of a world we create by our intentions and by our choices. We live in a world received from others, past and present, in a world we make our own, and a world which with others we shape for the future. Our contemporary world is inflicted with a deep-seated division. There is the "objectivity" and universality of technique and control and the "subjectivity" and isolation of the individual and his concerns. The escalation of scientific achievement has resulted in the manipulation, the privatizing, and even the negation of the community of subjects whose very self-transcending acts of knowledge and choice have created the sciences. Many are engaged today in analyzing and overcoming the division. A notable collaborator is Bernard Lonergan. His work is an effort to lead members of the contemporary community who are aware of the division both in themselves and in others to the healing recovery of themselves as subjects. His therapy leads to the recall of the potentiality and the actuality of the forms of human self-transcendence.

This study has presented key elements of Lonergan's praxis for recovery of the human subject. Persons in their structured intentional acts are method. All areas to which the mind and appetite apply themselves are united in the subjects who attend to them, who try to comprehend them, who confirm their comprehension, and who act on the basis of their knowledge. Persons become who they would be by what they choose to know and how they choose to live. Through *Insight* and its carefully tailored exercises, Lonergan leads his readers to understand and evaluate their own creative processes of understanding and evaluation. He leads to a further possession of one's own interiority through apprehension and affirmation of one's own interiority. Lonergan's particular reflection on reflection, his praxis of our praxis arises from and is directed to our own period of intellectual, social and consequent religious crisis. Lonergan's call and method for the recovery of the subject leads to the integration of interior and exterior and of subject with subject. The objects of knowledge and of choice include both one's world and one's self. And the construction of the world involves the creation of one's self. But as knowing is both cumulative and collaborative — as the sciences bear witness — so the construction of the world both physically and as an ambiance of meaning is the creation of subjects in community.

But what of religion? Subjects and communities not only grow and choose the good but decline and choose unwisely and with malice. Religion reaches to the core of the malady. It is the transformation of the hearts of those caught in the web of evil, their own and others'. It is the anchoring of the subject's willingness in the ultimately beyond the self. As such it is the foundation for altering the pattern of decline. For grounded in surrender to the Absolute, the self comes to see itself in proper relation to the world and to other selves. The various disguises of personal and communal egoisms are slowly penetrated and discarded. And the worth of understanding and creating a viable world is both recognized and implemented. Confirmed in affective bonds to the Ultimate, persons who are religious can value themselves and others anew and can recognize the possibility and challenge of forming or transforming the societies in which they live. Their own evil healed at the root, they can in the limit respond to the evil of others with good out of compassion[1] or out of love.[2]

Lonergan discloses religion at the deepest and the healing point of human desire. The desire to know and to do are the same trajectory. The liberation of knowing and doing to follow their own intrinsic dynamism is won at the point where doing becomes loving and being loved. And if the liberation is not won the healing itself is truncated. "Intrinsic to the nature of healing, there is the extrinsic requirement of a concomitant creative process. For just as the creative process, when unaccompanied by healing, is distorted and corrupted by bias, so too the healing process, when unaccompanied by creating, is a soul without a body."[3].

I think one only interprets Lonergan properly when one sees his own work of carefully describing and explaining the nexus of human consciousness in this time of a bifurcation of consciousness as part of the creative process which religious healing renders possible. For it is in no abstract context that Lonergan labors. He is a religious man faced with the dilemma of modern man. His own Christian faith is "a soul without a body" if inner healing does not liberate "a concomitant creative process" which in our own time can forge a link both intelligently and verifiably between the seeming diverse realms of economics and science, ethics and religion. Lonergan is acutely aware of the extent of the challenge to human survival that we face. It is to the resources of religion that he looks for basic healing. But it is from the resources of all our intelligence and creativity freed by basic healing, that he seeks enfleshment of that healing in society. He recalls poignantly what happened once before when that creativity was not forthcoming.

> Christianity developed and spread within the ancient empire of Rome. It possessed the spiritual power to heal what was unsound in that imperial domain. But it was unaccompanied by its natural complement of creating. So when the Roman empire decayed and disintegrated, the church indeed lived on. But it lived on, not in a civilized world, but in a dark and barbarous age in which, as a contemporary reported, men devoured one another as fishes in the sea.[4]

The creativity demanded is far more extensive than the elaboration of the structure of human intentionality. His own recent return to economic analysis makes clear how aware he is of this.[5] But in a period far more complex than ancient Rome, the therapeutic intellectual recovery by persons of the integral self-transcendence of their creating and of their healing can precisely be the necessary dynamic which unleashes both healing and creating.

But what of Christian theology and the dialogue of religions? Let us first consider two descriptions of theology which understand it as relating religion to a socio-cultural context. "A theology mediates between a cultural matrix and the significance and role of a religion in that matrix."⁶ In Robert Doran's fuller definition, "theology is the pursuit of accurate understanding regarding the moments of ultimacy in human experience, the referent of such moments, and their meaning for the individual and cultural life of humankind."⁷ Both are accurate descriptions as far as they go, but they risk an unfortunate oversight. For there is not only an object or set of objects of theological discourse, there is first of all a subject, the theologian, who reflects and mediates and who pursues accurate understanding. The moments of ultimacy, their referent, and their meaning for humankind are explored by a body-subject whose own history and consciousness are integral to his or her exploration. Both Lonergan and Doran are quite aware of this, all of their work promotes it, but their descriptions of theology unfortunately omit it. In an earlier cultural matrix, the person of the theologian was overlooked. In the historical development of knowledge, that is eminently understandable.⁸ Who the theologian was as a person established the context of his theology, but it was not culturally significant that he be aware of it. Today, however, the failure of the theologian to attend to his own subjectivity and historicity is both to "disregard or undermine the very conditions of . . . (the) emergence and existence"⁹ of his theology and also to negate the actual cultural context to which he is to mediate the significance and role of religion. Our cultural context is constituted by an awareness of historicity. It can neither be understood nor addressed by one who is unaware of his own historicity.¹⁰

Yet historical self-awareness though high achievement is insufficient for the theologian. Who he has become as a person, morally and religiously, establishes the only horizon from which he can understand the moments of ultimacy in human experience and their referent and therefore have any meaning to convey to the culture.

> The threefold conversion is, not a set of propositions that a theologian utters, but a fundamental and momentous change in the human reality that a theologian is. It operates, not by the simple process of drawing inferences from premises, but by changing the reality (his own) that the interpreter has to understand if he is to understand others, by changing the horizon within which the historian attempts to make the past intelligible, by changing the basic judgments of fact and of

> value that are found to be not positions but counter-positions...
>
> One's interpretation of others is affected by one's understanding of oneself, and the converted have a self to understand that is quite different from the self the unconverted have to understand...
>
> There is needed in the theologian the spiritual development that will enable him both to enter into the experience of others and to frame the terms and relations that will express that experience.[11]

The theologian in seeking the integration of moments of ultimacy and the cultural milieu is first of all, or at least concomitantly, seeking the integration of his own moments of ultimacy and his own milieu. If he has disregarded or fled his own limit experiences, there is nothing for him to integrate and he will hardly accurately perceive the need or the nature of the integration which others require. But this view of the theologian risks being static. The community to which a theologian belongs, the cultural context in which he lives, and he himself are constantly undergoing change. Self-transcendence is not a once and for all achievement. "Human authenticity is never some pure and serene and secure possession. It is ever a withdrawal from unauthenticity, and every successful withdrawal only brings to light the need for still further withdrawals."[12] What is required of the theologian is not some static spiritual perfection but radical openness to the realm of the Ultimate in his own experience, in the community of which he is a part, and in the community's scriptures and worship. Openness to the Transcendent is the beginning of authenticity on the religious level and already a form of its achievement. The theologian, like any believer, will grow as the ongoing limit experiences of life are faced, as the richness of his community and its tradition are comprehended and incorporated and as the quality of his life mediates meaning to his culture.

It should be clear that a theologian with access to his or her own spiritual, moral and intellectual resources has a significant contribution to make to the mediation of religion to a culture which is historically conscious. Such a theologian will understand religion itself as the ultimate self-transcendence of human subjectivity and will understand the dynamics of human creativity in relation to it. Perhaps the repetition of an earlier formulation is appropriate here.

The theologian aware within his own subjectivity of the cognitional principles which operate both in the sciences and in religion has also within himself the potential solution to the alienation of religion and the secular. For the theologian discovers within himself not an alienation *from* but an identity *with* the processes which when applied to various aspects of our universe have given rise to the sciences and the consequent secularization. Likewise, the possession within his own subjectivity of the religious horizon gives to the theologian potential access to the spirituality, the religious horizon of others, and can establish a common base for dialogue.[13]

The dialogue of religions as any dialogue is first based on what is shared. Even if what is shared cannot initially be articulated some presumption that there is indeed something in common seems necessary for dialogue to begin at all. Lonergan articulates what he considers to be shared among religious believers: all the levels of intentional consciousness and in particular a common openness to the Transcendent at the highest level of consciousness. And a substantial base this is. But the base is shared as infra-structure not as supra-structure. Although conscious, in the sense indicated earlier, it is not communally named. That naming is one of the tasks of interreligious dialogue. The conviction that there is something deeply in common to name is the starting point and impetus of dialogue.

> Religious experience does not occur with a label attached; of itself it is not formulated. To characterize it as infra-structure, however, regards only its relation to its formulation. But no means is it implied that it is inferior to any other experience or operation.
>
> Any formulation is in the context of some tradition and milieu; diverse formulations reflect different traditions; and as yet the world religions do not share some common theology or style of religious thinking.[14]

Although yet there is no "common theology or style of religious thinking" still what characterizes our time is the need and the desire and the anticipation of a communality at our root. The common root has been there. The outer and inner conditions necessary to explore it have not always been present. They are now.

We conclude on a note which both confirms and extends what we have written. Among the dialogues necessary for the renewing of

Christian foundational theology, the encounter with Marxism has taken on increasing importance and urgency. The same scientific and cultural crisis which traumatized Christians and the followers of other religious traditions has also been the seedbed for the Marxian critique of society and of religion. Marxists, Hindus, Buddhists, Jews, Moslems, Christians inhabit and interpret the same world. The encounter then already exists. The dialogue with Marxists provides a further and essential context for the development of Christian foundations. It must be seen as concomitant and complementary to dialogue with the living religions. The Marxist category of praxis calls for an existential reversal of the subordination of action to theory, in a way similar to the Lonerganian analysis of the priority of religious living over doctrine. The horizon shift provides a possible common basis for dialogue. The necessity for dialogue, at least from the Christian perspective, comes from the need to incorporate the Marxist insights into the social dimension of the human and human power over history into the liberating love which is the gift of religious conversion. Religious, ethical and historical-intellectual consciousness all have their center in the higher, more inclusive dimensions of our subjectivity. In every case, we are impoverished and fragmented when these dimensions develop in isolation. In our own time, human survival is at stake. The approach to religious foundations suggested in this study is pertinent then, we believe, to Marxist-Christian dialogue. Both Marxism and Lonerganian foundations arise from and are concerned with the liberation of the human subject. We are that human subject. It is our hopes that are at stake.

[13] Cf. Carrin Dunne, *Buddha and Jesus: Conversations* (Springfield, Illinois: Templegate Publishing Co., 1975), for a fascinating and perceptive example of inner dialogue after the manner of Jungian active imagination or Ignatian contemplation.

[14] M. (ed.), *The Gospel of Sri Ramakrishna*, trans. by Swami Nikhilananda (Madras: Sri Ramakrishna Math, 1969); Claude Stark, *God of All: Sri Ramakrishna's Approach to Religious Plurality* (Cape Cod: Claude Stark Inc., 1974), pp. 22-103.

[15] Panikkar, "The Emerging Myth," pp. 10-11.

[16] At their worst, religions foster alienation and secularism: "If in no other way at least from experience we have learnt that profession of zeal for the eternal salvation of souls does not make the persecution of heretics a means for the reconciliation of heretics. On the contrary, persecution leads to on-going enmity and in the limit to wars of religion. In like manner wars of religion have not vindicated religion; they have given color to a secularism that in the English-speaking world regards revealed religion as a merely private affair and in continental Europe thinks it an evil." Bernard Lonergan, "Healing and Creating in History," *Three Lectures* (Montreal: Thomas More Institute, 1975), pp. 64-65.

[17] "Again, while secularism has succeeded in making religion a marginal factor in human affairs, it has not succeeded in inventing a vaccine or providing some other antidote for hatred." Bernard Lonergan, "Healing," p. 64: cf. Bernard Lonergan, "The Absence of God in Modern Culture," *A Second Collection* (Philadelphia: The Westminster Press, 1974), pp. 101-16; William Lynch, *Christ and Prometheus* (Notre Dame: University of Notre Dame Press, 1970).

[18] Lonergan, "Healing," pp. 63-66.

[19] Bernard Lonergan, "Sacralization and Secularization" (unpublished address to Boston College Lonergan Workshop, Chestnut Hill, Massachusetts, June, 1974), p. 11.

[20] For reference to literature on this subject and for an insightful study of current economics and religion, cf. Matthew Lamb, "The Production Process and Exponential Growth: A Study in Socio-Economics and Theology" (unpublished paper delivered at Boston College Lonergan Workshop, Chestnut Hill, Massachusetts, June, 1975).

[21] Bernard Lonergan, "The Transition from a Classical World-View to Historical-Mindedness," *A Second Collection*, pp. 1-9; cf. also Lonergan, "Theology in its New Context," *A Second Collection*, pp. 55-67.

[22] Cf. Langdon Gilkey, *Naming the Whirlwind: The Renewal of God-Language* (New York: Bobbs-Merrill, 1969).

[23] Bernard Lonergan, *Method in Theology* (New York: Herder and Herder, 1972), p. 265 and *passim*.

[24] *Ibid.*, pp. 3-25.

[25] Bernard Lonergan, *Insight: A Study of Human Understanding* (New York: Philosophical Library, 1958), pp. 687-730.

[26] *Ibid.*, pp. xvii-xxx.

[27] Bernard Lonergan, "*Insight* Revisited," *A Second Collection*, p. 269.

[28] Lonergan, *Method*, p. 269.

[29] *Ibid.*, pp. 33-41.

[30] Bernard Lonergan, "Theology in its New Context," *A Second Collection*, p. 67.

[31] Lonergan, *Method*, pp. 105-67.

[32] *Ibid.*, pp. 108-109; cf. Dumoulin, *Christianity Meets Buddhism*, pp. 75-110.

[33] Lonergan, *Method*, p. 290; cf. also p. 270.

[34] *Ibid.*, pp. 235-66.

[35] *Ibid.*, pp. 267-93.

[36] *Ibid.*, p. 289.

[37] *Ibid.*, pp. 305-12.

[38] Bernard Lonergan, "The Subject," *A Second Collection*, p. 71.

Chapter 2

[1] Lonergan, *Method*, p. 3; cf. Lonergan's treatment of dialectical issues in scientific and philosophical method, *Insight*, pp. 402-30.

[2] Lonergan, *Method*, pp. 4-13.

[3] *Ibid.*, p. 4.

[4] Lonergan, *Insight*, p. 674. This quotation specifically refers to Lonergan's consideration of God.

[5] Lonergan, *Method*, p. 7.

[6] Lonergan, *Insight*, p. xxviii (italics Lonergan's) and p. 748.

[7] Matthew Lamb, "Wilhelm Dilthey's Critique of Historical Reason and Bernard Lonergan's Meta-Methodology" in *Language, Truth and Meaning*, ed. by Philip McShane (Notre Dame: University of Notre Dame Press, 1972), p. 125.

[8] Lonergan, *Method*, p. 231.

[9] *Ibid.*, p. 20.

[10] Lonergan, *Insight*, pp. 401-30.

[11] J. Eduardo Perez Valera has completed one such study in terms of Zen and Yoga in his doctoral dissertation, *Hacia Una Filosofia Transcultural* (Munchen-Pullach, 1971).

[12] Cf. Bernard Lonergan, "Cognitional Structure," *Collection* (New York: Herder and Herder, 1967), pp. 221-39 for an excellent summary presentation.

[13] Lonergan, *Method*, pp. 14-15.

[14] Bernard Lonergan, "Religious Studies and/or Theology." (The Donald Mathers Memorial Lectures presented at Queen's University, Kingston, Ontario, 1976), pp. 507.

[15] *Ibid.*, p. 6.

[16] Lonergan, *Method*, pp. 17-18; cf. also Lonergan, *Insight*, pp. 324-28.

[17] Lonergan, "Mission and the Spirit," *Concilium,* vol. 9, no. 10, p. 74.

[18] Lonergan, *Method*, pp. 6, 9 and 107.

[19] Bernard Lonergan, *The Philosophy of God and Theology* (Philadelphia: The Westminister Press, 1973), p. 38.

[20] Bernard Lonergan, "Religious Commitment" in *The Pilgrim People: A Vision With Hope*, ed. by Joseph Papin (Villanova: Villanova University Press, 1970), p. 51.

[21] Lonergan, *Insight*, pp. 401-30.

[22] *Ibid.*, p. 736.

[23] Lonergan, *Method*, p. 19. Lonergan's own shift in understanding of the notion of value from *Insight* to *Method* provides an excellent example of the possibilities for development without a radical reformulation of method; cf. *infra,* pp.41-45.

[24] Lonergan, *Method*, p. 13.

[25] *Ibid.*, pp. 22-23.

[26] Lonergan, *Insight*, pp. xxi-xxii.

[27] Lonergan, *Method*, p. xi.

[28] Cf. Lonergan, "The Transition from a Classicist World-View to Historical Mindedness," *A Second Collection*, pp. 1-10, for the context for this transposition.

[29] Lonergan, *Method*, p. 25.

[30] Lonergan, *Philosophy of God*, p. 33.

[31] Lonergan, *A Second Collection*, p. 170.

[32] Lonergan, *Insight*, pp. 320-28.

[33] Lonergan, "The Subject," *A Second Collection*, pp. 69-86.

[34] This last level of valuing is not fully differentiated by Lonergan from the previous cognitional levels till after *Insight*. In *Insight* valuing is in terms of knowing; the fourth level is the conscious subject "demanding conformity of his doing to his knowing," p. 613. Lonergan is there still straining for the view which will later acknowledge valuing as a transcendental level in its own right, just as truth is on the rational level, cf. *Method*, pp. 34-36; *A Second Collection*, p. 277; and "Truth and Value," *infra,* pp.41-45.

[35] Lonergan, *Insight*, p. 349.

[36] Lonergan, *Method*, p. 35.

[37] *Ibid.*, p. 51.

[38] *Ibid.*, p. 36; cf. Augustine's *Confessions*; cf. also John of the Cross, *The Collected Works of John of the Cross* (Washington: ICS Publications, 1973), pp. 617-37 on "the caverns of feeling."

[39] Lonergan's treatment of theological categories in terms of interiority analysis is developed *infra,* pp.63-66.

[40] Lonergan, *Method*, p. 29; cf. William Ernest Hocking, *The Meaning of God in Human Experience* (New Haven: Yale University Press, 1912), pp. 353-54.

[41] Lonergan, "The Possibility of Ethics, " *Insight*, pp. 595-633; Lonergan, "The Notion of Value," *Method*, pp. 34-41.

[42] Lonergan, "*Insight* Revisited," *A Second Collection*, p. 277; cf. also Frederick Crowe, "An Exploration of Lonergan's New Notion of Value," *Science et Esprit*, xxix (1977), pp. 123-44.

[43] Lonergan, *Insight*, p. 74.

[44] *Ibid.*, p. 9.

[45] Cf. *infra,* pp.45-49.

[46] Lonergan, *Insight*, pp. 624-25.

[47] Lonergan, *Method*, p. 104.

[48] *Ibid.*, pp. 47-52.

[49] Lonergan, "Religious Commitment," pp. 51-52.

[50] Lonergan, "The Response of the Jesuit as Priest and Apostle in the Modern World," *A Second Collection*, pp. 165-70. What the later Lonergan calls "authenticity" he treats earlier under the category of "genuineness," *Insight*, pp. 475-78. In both cases he sees the development of full human potential to be through progressive stages of self-transcendence.

[51] Lonergan, "The Response of the Jesuit," pp. 168-72.

[52] Lonergan, *Method*, p. 106.

[53] Lonergan, *Insight*, p. 185.

[54] Lonergan, *Method*, p. 103.

[55] Lonergan, *Philosophy of God*, pp. 11-14.

[56] Lonergan, *Method*, p. 116.

[57] Lonergan, *Philosophy of God*, p. 13.

[58] Lonergan, *Method*, p. 342. The first two questions are Lonergan's own treatment of the cosmological argument. They are fully developed in *Insight*, pp. 634-86.

[59] *Lonergan, Method*, p. 103.

[60] *Ibid.*

[61] Cf. Lonergan, *Insight*, pp. 627-33.

[62] Lonergan, *Method*, p. 101.

[63] Cf. Lonergan, *Method*, pp. 117-18; also Bernard Lonergan, "The Transition from a Classical World-View to Historical Mindedness," *A Second Collection*, pp. 7-9. For the major text, cf. Bernard Lonergan, *De Verbo Incarnato* (Rome: Gregorian University Press, 1964), pp. 552-93. Cf. also "Psyche, the Intentional Task, and the Cross," *infra,* pp.80-91.

[64] Lonergan, *Method*, p. 39.

[65] *Ibid.*, p. 29.

[66] *Ibid.*, pp. 115-16.

[67] Lonergan, *Method*, p. 38.

[68] Quoted in *Method*, p. 39.

[69] Lonergan, *Method*, p.40.

[70] *Ibid.*, pp. 30-34.

[71] *Ibid.*, p. 31.

[72] Bernard Lonergan, *"Mission and the Spirit," pp. 74-75.*

[73] Lonergan, *Method*, pp. 41-61.

[74] Lonergan, "Belief: Today's Issue," *A Second Collection*, pp. 87-99.

[75] Cf. Joachim Wach, *The Comparative Study of Religions* (New York: Columbia University Press, 1958), pp. 131-43.

[76] Lonergan, "Dimensions of Meaning,"*Collection*, pp. 254-55; cf. also *Method*, pp. 356-57.

[77] Lonergan, *Method*, p. 28.

[78] *Ibid.*, pp. 27-30 on Piaget.

[79] Lonergan, *Insight*, p. 175.

[80] *Ibid.*, p. 705; cf. also Lonergan, *Method*, pp. 43-44.

[81] Cf. Lonergan, *Method*, p. 223.

[82] Lonergan, *Insight*, pp. 713-18.

[83] Cf. Lonergan, "Healing," pp. 55-68; also Lonergan, *Insight*, pp. 234-35.

[84] Lonergan, *Insight*, p. xiv.

[85] Lonergan, *Method*, pp. 54-55.

[66] *Ibid.*, p. 55.

[67] Cf. Lonergan, *Insight*, pp. 191-206; 218-42; 627-33; 688-93.

[68] Lonergan, *Insight*, p. 623.

[69] Lonergan, "Healing," p. 63.

[90] Alfred North Whitehead, *Religion in the Making* (New York: New World Publishing Co., 1960), p. 16.

[91] Lonergan, *Method*, p. 243.

Chapter 3

[1] *Ibid*, p. 130.

[2] "General categories regard objects that come within the purview of other disciplines as well as theology." Lonergan, *Method*, p. 282.

[3] Lonergan, *Method*, pp. 286-87.

[4] "Special categories regard objects proper to theology." Lonergan, *Method*, p. 282.

[5] Lonergan, *Method*, pp. 104-5.

[6] Lonergan, *Method*, p.15.

[7] Lonergan, *Method*, p. 278.

[8] Lonergan, "Religious Commitment," pp. 45-46.

[9] Lonergan, *Method*, p. 106.

[10] Lonergan, *Method*, p. 282. Also cf. *Insight*, p. 568 and 736.

[11] Cf. *infra,* pp.67-68.

[12] Lonergan, *Method*, pp. 281-91.

[13] *Ibid.*, p. 281.

[14] *Ibid.*, p. 285.

[15] *Ibid.*, pp.286-87.

[16] *Ibid.*, pp. 282-83.

[17] *Ibid.*, pp. 108-18.

[18] *Ibid.*, p. 120; cf. also pp. 107 and 343.

[19] Raimundo Panikkar, "The Category of Growth in Comparative Religion: A Critical Self-Examination," *Harvard Theological Review*, LXVI (1973), p. 123.

[20] Lonergan, *Method*, pp. 106-07, 113, 123, 340.

[21] *Ibid.*, pp. 106, 341-42.

[22] *Ibid.*, pp. 29, 278, 341-42.

[23] *Ibid.*, pp. 106, 289.

[24] *Ibid.*, pp. 242, 273, 278, 341.

[25] *Ibid.*, pp. 106, 242.

[26] *Ibid.*, pp. 341, 350.

[27] *Ibid.*, p. 106.

[28] *Ibid.*

[29] *Ibid.*, pp. 29, 277, 341.

[30] Lonergan, "The Emerging Religious Consciousness of Our Time," p. 26.

[31] *Method*, p. 341.

[32] Lonergan, *"Mission and the Spirit,"* p. 77.

[33] Lonergan, "Religious Commitment," p. 47.

[34] *Ibid.*, p. 2; Lonergan, *Method*, pp. 106, 115.

[35] Lonergan, "Theology in its New Context," pp. 66-67.

[36] Lonergan, *Method*, p. 342.

[37] *Ibid.*, p. 77.

[38] *Ibid.*, p. 29; cf. also pp. 77, 273.

[39] *Ibid.*, p. 112.

[40] *Ibid.*, p. 273.

[41] *Ibid.*, pp. 59, 273.

[42] Lonergan, "Religious Commitment," p. 32. Note Lonergan's caution in making an affirmation about Buddhism. He is quite aware that he is not an historian of religions.

[43] Lonergan, *Method*, p. 110; cf. also Lonergan, "Religious Commitment," p. 31.

[44] Lonergan, *Method*, p. 292.

[45] *Method*, p. xii.

[46] Lonergan, "Faith and Beliefs," (unpublished, n.p., 1969), p. 1.

[47] Lonergan, *Method*, p. 343.

[48] Lonergan, *Philosophy of God*, p. 19.

[49] For Romans, Mark, and Deuteronomy, cf. *Method*, p. 105; cf. also "Faith and Beliefs," p. 5; "The Response of the Jesuit as Priest and Apostle in the Modern World," p. 171; "Religious Committment," p. 21; "Future of Christianity," p. 153; *Philosophy of God*, p. 9. Frederick Crowe points out the particular frequency of Romans 5:5 in almost all of Lonergan's recent papers, "Early Jottings on Bernard Lonergan's Method in Theology," *Science et Esprit*, XXV (1973), p. 131.

[50] Lonergan, "The Response of the Jesuit," p. 174.

[51] Lonergan, *Method*, p. 119; "Religious Commitment," p. 23.

[52] Lonergan, "Future of Christianity," p. 154.

[53] Lonergan, "Religious Commitment," pp. 24, 27, 28; "Faith and Beliefs," pp. 5, 7.

[54] Lonergan, "Religious Commitment," p. 22.

[55] Lonergan, "The Response of the Jesuit," p. 174.

[56] Lonergan, *Method*, p. 278.

[57] *Ibid.*, pp. 108-9; "Faith and Beliefs," pp. 6-7.

[58] Lonergan, "Religious Commitment," p. 47.

[59] Published as *Grace and Freedom*, ed. by J. Patout Burns (New York: Herder and Herder, 1971).

[60] Cf. pp. 37-38 *supra*, for a discussion of the priority of cognitional analysis over metaphysics. "Religious Commitment," pp. 4-7 has a useful summary of the transition from medieval to modern categories.

[61] Lonergan, *Method*, pp. 288-89.

[62] Lonergan, "Religious Commitment," pp. 26-7.

[63] Lonergan, *Method*, p. 282.

[64] *Ibid.*, p. 350.

[65] Paul Ricoeur, *Freud and Philosophy*, translated by Denis Savage (New Haven: Yale University Press, 1970), p. 28.

[66] Cf. Daisetz Suzuki, *Japanese Spirituality* (Japan: Japan Society for the Promotion of Science, 1972); Swami Nikhilananda, "The Realistic Aspect of Indian Spirituality," in *The Indian Mind*, ed. by Charles Moore (Honolulu: University of Hawaii Press, 1967), pp. 216-47; Seyyed Hossein Nasr, "The Spiritual States in Sufism," *Sufi Essays* (Albany: State University of New York Press, 1972), pp. 68-83; John-David Robinson (ed.) *Word out of Silence: A Symposium on World Spiritualities, Cross Currents* XXIV (Summer-Fall, 1974).

[67] Suzuki, *Japanese Spirituality*, p. 99.

Chapter 4

¹ Lonergan, *Method*, p. 77. (Italics added.)

² Max Scheler, *Ressentiment*, edited by Lewis Coser (New York: Schocken Books, 1976).

³ Erich Neumann, *The Great Mother: An Analysis of the Archetype*, translated by Ralph Manheim (Princeton, New Jersey: Princeton University Press, 1972).

⁴ Although I recognized the lacuna in Lonergan's thought of a specific category of psychic conversion concomitantly with Rev. Robert Doran, I owe to him the development and articulation of the elements of psychic conversion and the exploration of its foundational significance. Cf. Robert Doran, *Subject and Psyche: Ricoeur, Jung, and the Search for Foundations* (Washington, D.C.: The University Press of America, 1977).

⁵ Robert Doran, *Subject and Psyche: Ricoeur, Jung, and the Search for Foundations* (Washington, D.C.: University Press of America, 1977). Cf. Carl Jung, *Memories, Dreams, Reflections*, edited by Aniela Jaffe (New York: Vintage Books, 1963), pp. 216-17; George Widengren, "The Principle of Evil in the Eastern Religions," in *Evil*, edited by the Curatorium of the C.G. Jung Institute, Zurich (Evanston: Northwestern University Press, 1967), pp. 19-55.

⁶ Carl Jung, "Answer to Job," *The Collected Works of Carl Jung*, translated by R.F.C. Hull (Princeton: Princeton University Press, 1973) XI, pp. 355-470. This same interpretation is followed by Edward Edinger, *Ego and Archtype* (New York: G.P. Putnam's Sons, 1972), pp. 76-96.

⁷ Jung, "Answer to Job," p. 419.

⁸ Presented in a seminar on *Insight*, Marquette University, 1976.

⁹ Carl Jung, *Memories, Dreams, Reflections*, edited by Aniela Jaffe (New York: Vintage Books, 1963), p. 219.

¹⁰ Sebastian Moore, *The Crucified Jesus is no Stranger* (New York: The Seabury Press, 1977).

¹¹ Cf. Bernard Lonergan, *De Verbo Incarnato*, 3rd ed., rev. (Rome: Gregorian University Press, 1964), pp. 552-93. For a thorough study of Lonergan's soteriology of the cross, cf. William Loewe, *Toward the Critical Mediation of Theology: A Development of the Soteriological Theme in the Work of Bernard Lonergan* (unpublished Ph.D. dissertation, Marquette University, 1974); cf. also Loewe's "Lonergan and the Law of the Cross: A Universalist View of Salvation," *Anglican Theological Review*, LIX (April, 1977), pp. 162-74.

¹² Edward Edinger, *Ego and Archetype* (New York: G.P. Putnam's Sons, 1972), p. 131; cf. also Carl Jung, *Memories, Dreams, Reflections* (New York: Random House, 1963), p. 338.

¹³ Moore, *The Crucified Jesus*, p. xi. Moore's distinction that evil becomes sin when confronted with the Crucified is consistent with Lonergan's more generally expressed position that with "an apprehension of the divinely ordained order of the universe . . . wrong-doing takes on the character of sin against God." *Insight*, p. 666.

[14] Jung, *Memories, Dreams, Reflections*, pp. 347-48.

[15] Edinger, *Ego and Archetype*, p. 15.

[16] Cf. Doran, *Subject and Psyche*, p. 21, foot-note 9.

[17] Moore, *The Crucified Jesus*, p. 8.

[18] Lonergan, *Insight*, p. 667.

[19] *Ibid.*

[20] *Ibid.*, p. 666.

[21] Moore, *The Crucified Jesus*, p. 35.

[22] Lonergan, *Insight*, p. 666.

[23] Moore, *The Crucified Jesus*, pp. 33-34.

[24] "What is basic sin? It is the irrational. Why does it occur? If there were a reason, it would not be sin. There may be excuses; there may be extenuating circumstances; but there cannot be a reason for basic sin consists, not in yielding to reasons and reasonableness, but in failing to yield to them; it consists not in inadvertent failure but in advertence to and in acknowledgement of obligation that, none the less, is not followed by reasonable response." Lonergan, *Insight*, p. 667.

[25] *Ibid.*, pp. 667-8.

[26] *Ibid.*, p. 668.

[27] Jung, "Answer to Job," pp. 377-86; cf. also David Burrell, *Exercises in Religious Understanding* (Notre Dame: University of Notre Dame Press, 1974), pp. 222-32, for a similar critique of Jung. Burrell shows how from Jung's own perspective evil may be understood as the privation of good and therefore to find the cause of evil in God is unwarranted. "Jung's own discussion of *individuation* had already suggested a context within which 'good' and 'evil' play their assessment roles. The alternative to undertaking the inner journey . . . is not to take another journey . . . but simply to fail to do it . . . At this level evil appears as a failure, a want, a privation, and not as an active and symmetric opposite. The result, of course is both tenacious and destructive, for it is to be gripped by the illusion that we *know* what we are up to when in fact we do not." *Ibid.*, p. 228.

[28] Moore, *The Crucified Jesus is No Stranger*, p. x.

[29] *Ibid.*

[30] *Ibid.*

[31] *Ibid.*, p. xi.

[32] *Ibid.*, p. xii.

[33] *Ibid.*, pp. 8-9.

[34] *Ibid.*, p. 37.

[35] *Ibid.*, p. 55.

[37] *Ibid.*, pp. 8-9.

[37] *Ibid.*, p. xi.

[38] *Ibid.*, p. 10.

[39] *Ibid.*, p. 11.

[40] *Ibid.*

[41] *Ibid.*

[42] *Ibid.*, p. xii.

[43] Cf. Bernard Lonergan, "Christology Today," *Le Christ Hier, Aujourd 'hui et Demain* (Quebec: Les Presses de L'Universite Laval, 1976).

[44] Bernard Lonergan, "Theological Understanding," translated (unpublished) by F.P. Greaney from *Divinarum Personarum Conceptio Analogica* (Rome: Gregorian University, 1957).

[45] Lonergan, "The Future of Christianity," *A Second Collection*, pp. 149-63.

[46] Lonergan, "Faith and Beliefs" (unpublished, n.p., 1969).

[47] Lonergan, "The Response of the Jesuit, as Priest and Apostle in the Modern World," *A Second Collection*, pp. 168-87.

[48] "I must point out that my model is just a skeleton. To apply it to any particular religion, further parts may need to be added. Moreover, because religions can differ in fundamental ways, one must have different sets of parts to add and even one may have to add them in quite different ways." Lonergan, "Faith and Beliefs," p. 10.

[49] Lonergan, "Prolegomena to the Study of the Emerging Religious Consciousness of our Time," (address delivered in Vienna, Austria, January, 1975).

[50] Lonergan, "Future of Christianity," p. 149.

[51] *Ibid.*, pp. 149-51; cf. Friedrich Heiler, "The History of Religions as a Preparation for the Cooperation of Religions," in *The History of Religions: Essays in Methodology*, pp. 142-53.

[52] Lonergan, "Future of Christianity," p. 151.

[53] "Now I have been quoting St. Paul and St. Augustine and speaking in Christian terms, but I have not been doing so in any exclusive manner, for it is not Christian doctrine that the gift of God's love is restricted to Christians." Lonergan, "The Future of Christianity," p. 155.

[54] Lonergan, "Future of Christianity," p. 156.

[55] "In the Christian, accordingly, God's gift of his love is a love that is in Christ Jesus. From this fact flow the social, historical, doctrinal aspects of Christianity." "The Future of Christianity," p. 156.

[56] *Ibid.*

[57] *Ibid.*

[58] *Ibid.*

[59] The community of redemption will itself be subject to all the aberrations that in fact call for redemption, cf. Lonergan, *Insight*, p. 722. The saving community leaves freedom intact.

[60] Cf. footnote 11 of this chapter.

[61] Lonergan, "Future of Christianity," p. 159.

[62] *Ibid.*, p. 159-61.

[63] *Ibid.*, p. 161.

[64] *Ibid.*, p. 162-63.

[65] Cf. Lonergan, "The Word," *Method*, pp. 112-15. "Word" is a general category which can be applied to any carrier of meaning.

[66] Lonergan, "Faith and Beliefs," p. 1.

[67] *Ibid.* Cf. also *Method*, pp. 115-19.

[68] Lonergan, "Faith and Beliefs," p. 1.

[69] *Ibid.*, p. 2.

[70] *Ibid.*

[71] *Ibid.*, p. 7.

[72] "I think that many of you will grant that a basic component of religious involvement among Christians is God's gift of his love. But I wish to indicate a reason for thinking that the same may be said of religious involvement in all the world religions, in Christianity, Judaism, Islam, Zoroastrian Mazdaism, Hinduism, Buddhism, Taoism. For Fredrich Heiler has described at some length seven common areas in those religions." Lonergan, "Faith and Beliefs," p. 12.

[73] Lonergan, "Faith and Beliefs," p. 14.

[74] *Ibid.*

[75] *Ibid.*, p. 15.

[76] *Ibid.*

[77] *Ibid.*

[78] *Ibid.*, pp. 17-19.

[79] "As sociologists insist, such a world is constructed not individually but socially. As theorists of historicity would add, it is not the work of a generation but of the ages." *Ibid.*, p. 19.

[80] Lonergan, "Faith and Beliefs," p. 20.

[81] *Ibid.*, pp. 20-31.

[82] *Ibid.*, p. 21.

[63] *Ibid.*

[64] Lonergan, "The Response of the Jesuit," pp. 165-70.

[65] *Ibid.*, pp. 170-73.

[66] *Ibid.*, pp. 172-73.

[67] *Ibid.*, pp. 173-75.

[68] *Ibid.*, pp. 175-81.

[69] *Ibid.*, pp. 181-82.

[90] *Ibid.*, pp. 183-87.

[91] *Ibid.*, p. 174.

[92] *Ibid.*, p. 181.

[93] Wilfred Cantwell Smith, "Comparative Religion: Whither — and Why?" in *The History of Religions: Essays in Methodology*, ed. by Mircea Eliade and Joseph M. Kitagawa (Chicago: The University of Chicago Press, 1959), p. 34.

[94] Cf. Bernard Lonergan, "Religious Studies and/or Theology;" Joachim Wach, "The Place of the History of Religions in the Study of Theology," *Types of Religious Experience* (Chicago: The University of Chicago Press, 1951); Smith, "Comparative Religion."

[95] Smith, "Comparative Religion," pp. 44-45.

[96] Wach, "The History of Religions," pp. 27-29.

[97] Joseph Kitagawa, "The History of Religions in America," *The History of Religions*, p. 15.

[98] These questions particularly relate to the goals of the first three levels of consciousness, experience, understanding and judgment. The disciplines with these goals Lonergan calls, respectively, Research, Interpretation and History; cf. Lonergan, *Method*, pp. 149-234.

[99] Decisional questions relate to the goals of the fourth level of consciousness. Lonergan calls the disciplines which explore these questions Dialectics and Foundations. Dialectics evaluates the past, Foundations expresses the value positions now chosen; cf. Lonergan, *Method*, pp. 235-93.

[100] "While these commitments are bound to color his understanding to some extent, he can make an effort to distinguish in his own mind between his commitments and his attempts to understand the conscious response of others. On the other hand, the illusion of complete non-involvement, with all the deceptions it nourishes, is more detrimental to objectivity than a lively sense of involvement controlled by the desire to understand." Benjamin Swartz as cited in Kitagawa, "The History of Religions in America," p. 28.

[101] Lonergan, "Religious Studies," pp. 54-58.

[102] Lonergan, *Method*, pp. 267-71.

[103] Lonergan, "Religious Studies," p. 65.

[104] *Ibid.*

[105] Lonergan, *Method*, p. 268.

[106] *Ibid.*

[107] *Ibid.*

[108] *Ibid.*

[109] *Ibid.*, p. 131.

[110] *Ibid.*, p. 236.

[111] *Ibid.*, p. 237.

[112] Bernard Lonergan, "Natural Right and Historical Mindedness" (unpublished, n.p., 1976) p. 20.

[113] *Ibid.*

[114] Smith, "Comparative Religion," p. 34.

Chapter 5

[1] "A Bodhisattava resolves: I take upon myself the burden of all suffering. I am resolved to do so. I will endure it. I do not turn or run away, do not tremble, am not terrified, nor afraid, do not turn back or despond . . . And why? Because it is surely better that I alone should be in pain than that all these beings should fall into the state of woe." From a Mahayana sutra in *The Compassionate Buddha*, ed. by E.A. Burtt (New York: New American Library, 1955), pp. 133-34.

[2] Matthew 5:43-48; Romans 5:6-11.

[3] Lonergan, "Healing," p. 65.

[4] *Ibid.*, p. 65.

[5] "From economic theorists we have to demand, along with as many other types of analysis as they please, a new and specific type that reveals how moral precepts have both a basis in economic process and so an effective application to it. From moral theorists we have to demand, along with their other various forms of wisdom and prudence, specifically economic precepts that arise out of economic process itself and promote its proper functioning." Lonergan, "Healing and Creating in History," *Three Lectures*, pp. 65-66.

[6] Lonergan, *Method*, p. xi.

[7] Robert Doran, "Aesthetics and the Opposites," *Thought* LII (June, 1977), pp. 117-33.

[8] Lonergan, "The Transition from a Classicist World-View to Historical Mindedness," and "Theology in a New Context," *A Second Collection*, pp. 1-10 and pp. 55-67; cf. also *Method*, pp. 253-65 and pp. 86-96.

[9] Lonergan, "The Subject," *A Second Collection*, p. 71.

[10] Certainly most in our culture do not have historical mindedness. They too are to have the gospel preached to them. Historical consciousness is not needed on the part of the theologian to mediate meaning to their culture. There are those who do possess historical mindedness, however, and they establish our broader cultural context. To fail to incorporate their values and to address their concerns is to fail the gospel; cf. Lonergan, *Method*, pp. 326-28.

[11] Lonergan, *Method*, pp. 270-71; p. 290; cf. also pp. 285-86.

[12] *Ibid.*, p. 110.

[13] *Supra,* p.12.

[14] Lonergan, "Prolegomena," p. 25.

Bibliography

Becker, Ernest. *The Denial of Death*. New York: The Free Press, 1973.

Burrell, David B. *Exercises in Religous Understanding*. Notre Dame: University of Notre Dame Press, 1974.

Campbell, Joseph. *The Masks of God: Oriental Mythology*. New York: Viking Press, 1972.

Conze, Edward. *Buddhism: Its Essence and Development*. New York: Harper & Row, 1964.

Conze, Edward. Editor. *Buddhist Texts Through the Ages*. New York: Harper & Row, 1964.

Doran, Robert. *Subject and Psyche: Ricoeur, Jung and the Search for Foundations*. Washington, D.C.: The University Press of America, 1977.

Dumoulin, Heinrich. *Christianity Meets Buddhism*. LaSalle, Illinois: Open Court Publishing Co., 1974.

Dunne, Carrin. *Buddha and Jesus: Conversations*. Springfield, Illinois: Templegate Publishing Co., Springfield, Illinois: Templegate Publishing Co., 1975.

Dunne, John S. *The Way of All the Earth*. New York: The MacMillan Co., 1972.

Edinger, Edward. *Ego and Archetype*. New York: G.P. Putnam's Sons, 1972.

Gilkey, Langdon. *Naming the Whirlwind: The Renewal of God-Language*. New York: Bobbs-Merrill, 1969.

Griffiths, Bede. *Return to the Center*. Springfield, Illinois: Templegate, 1977.

Hocking, William Ernest. *Living Religions and a World Faith.* New York: The MacMillan Co., 1940.

Hocking, William Ernest. *The Meaning of God in Human Experience.* New Haven: Yale University Press, 1912.

John of the Cross. *The Collected Works of John of the Cross.* Washington: ICS Publications, 1973.

Johnston, William. *The Still Point: Reflections on Zen and Christian Mysticism.* New York: Harper & Row, 1971.

Jung, Carl. *Memories, Dreams, Reflections.* Edited by Aniela Jaffe. New York: Vintage Books, 1963.

Klostermaier, Klaus. *In the Paradise of Krishna: Hindu and Christian Seekers.* Philadelphia: The Westminster Press, 1969.

Loewe, William. *Toward the Critical Mediation of Theology: A Development of the Soteriological Theme in the Work of Bernard Lonergan.* Unpublished Ph.D. Dissertation, Marquette University, 1974.

Lonergan, Bernard. *Grace and Freedom.* New York: Herder and Herder, 1971.

Lonergan, Bernard. *De Verbo Incarnato*, 3rd edition rev. Rome: Gregorian University Press, 1964.

Lonergan, Bernard. *Insight: A Study of Human Understanding.* New York: Philosophical Library, 1958.

Lonergan, Bernard. *Method in Theology.* New York: Herder and Herder, 1972.

Lynch, William. *Christ and Prometheus.* Notre Dame: University of Notre Dame Press, 1970.

Moore, Sebastian. *The Crucified Jesus is no Stranger.* New York: The Seabury Press, 1977.

Neumann, Erich. *The Great Mother: An Analysis of the Archetype.* Translated by Ralph Manheim. Vol. XLVII of the Bollingen Series. Princeton, New Jersey: Princeton University Press, 1972.

Neumann, Erich. *The Origins and History of Consciousness.* Translated by R.F.C. Hull. Vol. XLII of the Bollingen Series. Princeton University Press, 1969.

Organ, Troy Wilson. *Hinduism: Its Historical Development.* Woodbury, New York: Barron's Educational Series, Inc., 1974.

Panikkar, Raimundo. *The Trinity and the Religious Experience of Man.* New York: Orbis Books, 1973.

Perez-Valera, J. Eduardo. *Hacia Una Filosofia Trans-cultural.* Unpublished Ph.D. Dissertation, Munchen-Pullach, 1971.

Ramakrishna. *The Gospel of Sri Ramakrishna.* Edited by M. and translated by Swami Nikhilananda. Madras: Sri Ramakrishna Math, 1969.

Ricoeur, Paul. *The Symbolism of Evil.* Translated by Emerson Buchanan. Boston: Beacon Press, 1967.

Ricoeur, Paul. *Freud and Philosophy: An Essay on Interpretation.* Translated by Denis Savage. New Haven: Yale University Press, 1970.

Robertson, John-David, ed. *Word Out of Silence: A Symposium on World Spiritualities. Cross Currents,* XXIV (Summer-Fall, 1974.)

Samartha, S.J. and Taylor, J.B., eds. *Christian-Muslim Dialogue.* Geneva: World Council of Churches, 1973.

Scheler, Max. *Ressentiment.* Edited by Lewis Coser. New York: Schocken Books, 1976.

Speaking of Siva. Translated by A.K. Ramanujan. Baltimore: Penguin Books, Inc., 1973.

Stark, Claude. *God of All: Sri Ramakrishna's Approach to Religious Plurality.* Cape Cod, Massachusetts: Claude Stark, Inc., 1974.

Stevenson, W. Taylor. *History as Myth.* New York: The Seabury Press, 1969.

Suzuki, Daisetz. *Japanese Spirituality.* Japan: Japan Society for the Promotion of Science, 1972.

Suzuki, Daisetz. *Mysticism, Christian and Buddhist.* New York: Harper & Row, 1971.

Tracy, David. *Blessed Rage for Order.* New York: The Seabury Press, 1975.

The Upanishads. Translated by Swami Prabhavananda and Frederick Manchester. New York: New American Library, 1948.

Vatican Secretariat for Non-Christians. *For a Dialogue With Hinduism.* Rome: Editrice Ancora, 1971.

Vatican Secretariat for Non-Christians. *Toward the Meeting of Religions.* Boston: Daughters of St. Paul, 1967.

Wach, Joachim. *The Comparative Study of Religions.* New York: Columbia University Press, 1958.

Wach, Joachim. *Sociology of Religion.* Chicago: The University of Chicago Press, 1944.

Wach, Joachim. *Types of Religious Experience, Christian and Non-Christian.* University of Chicago Press, 1951.

Whitehead, Alfred North. *Religion in the Making.* New York: New World Publishing Co., 1960.

Whitson, Robley Edward. *The Coming Convergence of World Religions.* New York: Newman Press, 1971.

Zaehner, Robert C., ed. *The Bhagavad-Gita, with a Commentary Based on the Original Sources.* New York: Oxford University Press, 1973.

Zaehner, Robert C., ed. *Hinduism.* New York: Oxford University Press, 1972.

Zimmer, Heinrich. *Myths and Symbols in Indian Art and Civilization.* Edited by Joseph Campbell. Princeton: Princeton University Press, 1972.

Zimmer, Heinrich. *Philosophies of India.* Edited by Joseph Campbell. Princeton: Princeton University Press, 1971.

Articles

Doran, Robert. "Aesthetics and the Opposites," *Thought,* LII (June, 1977), 117-33.

Gregson, Vernon. "Chinese Wisdom and Ignatian Discernment," *Review for Religious,* XXXIII (July, 1974), 828-35.

Heiler, Friedrich. "The History of Religions as a Preparation for the Co-operation of Religions." *The History of Religions: Essays in Methodology.* Edited by Mircea Eliade and Joseph M. Kitagawa. Chicago: University of Chicago Press, 1959.

Jung, Carl. "Answer to Job." *The Collected Works of Carl Jung.* Translated by R. F. C. Hull. Vol. XI. Princeton: Princeton University Press, 1973.

Kitagawa, Joseph. "The History of Religions in America." *The History of Religions: Essays in Methodology.* Edited by Mircea Eliade and Joseph M. Kitagawa. Chicago: University of Chicago Press, 1959.

Lamb, Matthew. "The Production Process and Exponential Growth: A Study in Socio-Economics and Theology." Paper presented at Boston College Lonergan Workshop, Chestnut Hill, Massachusetts, June, 1975.

Lamb, Matthew. "Wilhelm Dilthey's Critique of Historical Reason and Bernard Lonergan's Meta-Methodology." *Language, Truth and Meaning.* Edited by Phillip McShane. Notre Dame: University of Notre Dame Press, 1972.

Loewe, William. "Lonergan and the Law of the Cross: A Universalist View of Salvation." *Anglican Theological Review,* LIX (April, 1977), 162-74.

Lonergan, Bernard. "The Absence of God in Modern Culture." *A Second Collection.* Philadelphia: The Westminster Press, 1974.

Lonergan, Bernard. "Christology Today: Methodological Reflections," *Le Christ Hier, Aujourd'hui et Demain.* Quebec: Les Presses de L'Universite Laval, 1976.

Lonergan, Bernard. "Cognitional Structure." *Collection.* New York: Herder and Herder, 1967.

Lonergan, Bernard. "Healing and Creating in History." *Three Lectures*. Montreal: Thomas More Institute, 1975.

Lonergan, Bernard. "*Insight* Revisited." *A Second Collection*.

Lonergan, Bernard. "Mission and the Spirit." *Experience of the Spirit*. (*Concilium* Vol. 9. No. 10). New York: Seabury Press, 1976.

Lonergan, Bernard. "Natural Right and Historical Mindedness." Paper presented at Boston College Lonergan Workshop, Chestnut Hill, Massachusetts, June, 1975.

Lonergan, Bernard. "Faith and Beliefs." Unpublished paper, n.p., 1969 (Mimeographed).

Lonergan, Bernard. "Prolegomena to the Study of the Emerging Religious Consciousness of our Time." Paper presented at the Second International Symposium on Belief, Vienna, Austria, January, 1975. *Studies in Religion/ Sciences Religieuses* 9, 1980.

Lonergan, Bernard. "Religious Commitment." *The Pilgrim People: A Vision With Hope*. Edited by Joseph Papin. Villanova: Villanova University Press, 1970.

Lonergan, Bernard. "Religious Studies and / or Theology." The Donald Mathers Memorial Lectures. Presented at Queens University, Kingston, Ontario, 1976. (Mimeographed).

Lonergan, Bernard. "The Future of Christianity." *A Second Collection*.

Lonergan, Bernard. "The Response of the Jesuit as Priest and Apostle in the Modern World." *A Second Collection*.

Lonergan, Bernard. "Sacralization and Secularization." Paper presented at Boston College Lonergan Workshop, Chestnut Hill, Massachusetts, June, 1975.

Lonergan, Bernard. "The Subject." *A Second Collection*.

Lonergan, Bernard. "Theological Understanding." *Divinarum Personarum Conceptio Analogica*. Rome: Gregorian University Press, 1957.

Lonergan, Bernard. "The Transition from a Classicist World-View to Historical Mindedness." *A Second Collection*.

Nasr, Seyyed Hossein. "The Spiritual States in Sufism." *Sufi Essays*. Albany: State University of New York Press, 1972.

Nikhilananda Swami. "The Realistic Aspect of Indian Spirituality." *The Indian Mind*. Edited by Charles Moore. Honolulu, Hawaii: University of Hawaii Press, 1967.

Panikkar, Raimundo. "The Category of Growth in Comparative Religion: A Critical Self-Examination." *Harvard Theological Review*, LXVI (January, 1973), 113-40.

Panikkar, Raimundo. "The Emerging Myth." *Monchanin*, VIII (June-December, 1975), 8-11.

Smith, Wilfred Cantwell. "Comparative Religion: Whither - and Why?" *The History of Religions: Essays in Methodology*. Edited by Mircea Eliade and Joseph M. Kitagawa. Chicago: University of Chicago Press, 1959.

Wach, Joachim. "The Place of the History of Religions in the Study of Theology." *Types of Religious Experience, Christian and non-Christian*. Chicago: The University of Chicago Press, 1951.

Widengren, George. "The Principle of Evil in the Eastern Religions." *Evil, Essays by Carl Kerenyi and Others*. Translated by Ralph Manheim and Hildegard Nagel. Edited by the Curatorium of the C. G. Jung Institute, Zurich. Evanston, Illinois: Northwestern University Press, 1967.

Index

Absolute, as term for God or the transcendent, 42;
see also God; Transcendent; Ultimate
Acts of The Apostles, 20
Adam, 90
Affect/ Affectivity, 80-81;
see also Feeling(s)
Alienation, 55, 90, 126;
see also Bias; Sin
Antecedent willingness and unwillingness, 55-56
Anthropology, 96
Aquinas, Thomas, 73;
see also Thomistic synthesis
Aristotelian,
philosophy, 37;
science, 8, 19, 23;
see also Aristotle
Aristotle, 8, 23, 43;
see also Aristotelian
Atheist, 73
Augustine, 50, 129, 136
Authenticity, 73, 81, 103, 129;
and inauthenticity, 44, 71, 121;
see also Self-transcendence

Belief, and faith, 97-100
Bhagavad-Gita, 48
Bias,
four forms of, 55;
(see also Alienation)
Bodhisattava, 139
Buddha, 48;
four noble truths of, 20
Buddhism, 3, 31, 123, 132, 137;
as a religion of spirituality, 16, 19-21, 76;
as atheistic mysticism, 70;
Mahayana, 67, 139;
Zen, 127
Burrell, David, 136

Christianity,
and ecclesiastical divisions, 20-21;
and experience of grace, 72-75, 98;
and Jungian psychology, 84-85;
and secularization, 7-9;
as religious community, 94-95;
distinctiveness (uniqueness) of, 91-103;
historical aspects of, 95-96, 119;
language special to, 63, 67-68, 70-71;
Lonergan's treatment of, 48;
see also Theology (Christian)
Cogniton,
analysis of, 10-11, 29-31
Cognitional theory, see Transcendental method
Community, 51-52; see also Christianity (as religious community);
Theologian (as member of a faith community).
Conscience, 15, 32
Conscious operations,
and community, 52;
explanation of, 10-15, 29-33, 38-41;
heuristic structure of 12;
normative (cross-cultural) character of, 33-36;
self-verification (self-identification) of, 10-11, 24-25, 30-33;
sublation of, 98
Consciousness,
as awareness, 39;
attending to, 39;
divisions (dichotomies) of, 14, 77, 117-119;
historical, 14, 96, 105, 107, 111, 120; 140;
modern, 117-119;
moral, 31-32, 41-45, (see also Value);
narcissism of, 86;
religious (see Religious interiority);
scientific, 8-9, 14, 105, 107, (see also Religion (and science);
Science(s)
Contemplation,
Ignatian, 126
Conversion,
as influencing conscious horizons,

149

111-113;
Christian, 84, 91;
psychic (and its relation to religious interiority), 80-91, 134;
religious, 56-57, 59, 71, 74-76, 99, 120-122;
threefold (intellectual, moral, religious), 56-57, 71, 99, 120-122
Corinthians, First (I), 72
Cosmology, 96
Creativity, *see* Progress
Cross, 84-85, 89; *see also* Jesus Christ
Crowe, Frederick, 129, 134
Crucified, *see* Jesus Christ
Culture,
classical and modern, 52, 95-96;
development of lower and higher, 52

Death, 89
Decision (fourth level of consciousness), 15, 31-32, 40
Decline, 50, 54-57, 118
Descartes, 18, 53
Deuteronomy, 72
Dialectics,
and dialogue, 113-115;
and the need of conversion (authenticity), 111-113;
horizon of, 110-113
Dialogue,
among religions, 1-2, 4, 14, 76, 104, 122; *see also* Religions (encounter among);
and dialectics, 113-115;
inner, 126;
Marxist-Christian, 123
Disciplines,
collaboration among, 31;
parity among, 23-24
Divine, *see* God; Transcendent; Ultimate
Doctrine(s),
as derivative of the experiential foundations of religion, 16, 17-18, 64-65, 76, 94-96
Doran, Robert, 82-83, 120, 136
Doubt, universal, 53-54
Dumoulin, Heinrich, 1, 127
Dunne, Carrin, 126

East,
and applicability of transcendental method, 33-34;
and mystics, 70;
and secularization, 7-8, 14;
and understanding of the 'spiritual', 76;
as challenge and aid to Christian theologian, 20;
traditions of, 28, 115
Edinger, Edward, 85, 134 &135
Ego,
and self, 84-85, 89-90
Eliade, Mircea, 125, 139
Epistemology, 37-38, 73
Error, 54
Evil,
and God's goodness, 82-83, 86-90, 134 &135;
and self-transcendence, 85-90;
as moral impotence, 48;
experience of, 47-48;
healing of, 118, 86-90;
physical and moral, 88;
see also Sin
Experience (first level of consciousness), 29-32, 39

Faculty psychology, 37-38
Faith,
and belief, 97-100;
in relation to history of religions and theology, 104-110;
universal character of, 97, 137
Feeling(s),
and value, 49-51;
identification of, 60;
intentional, 51;
non-intentional, 50-51;
see also Affect
Forgiveness, *see* Redemption
Freedom,
and God's goodness, 87-88;
intentional horizon of, 15, 31-32, 55-56
Freud, Sigmund, 8

Galatians, 72
Galilei, Galileo, 8
Gilkey, Langdon, 126
God,
and Christian religion, 93-96, 98-100, 136;
as name among different designations for religious interiority, 63-69;
as source of conversion, 57;
as supreme value, 50;
desire for, 45-49;
goodness of, 82-83, 86-90;
grace of, 72-74;
mystical experience of, 69-71;
openness to, 42-45;
see also Transcendent; Ultimate
Good, *see* Value
Grace,
as special theological category, 64-65,

72-75, 102;
as universally experienced, 73;
Christian experience of, 94-96
Growth, 50; *see also* Progress

Heiler, Friedrich, 73, 93, 94, 98, 125, 137
Hildebrand, Dietrich von, 50
Hinduism, 3, 123, 137;
as a religion of spirituality, 16, 19-21, 76;
Bhakti, 67
Historians of religion, 21;
and study of religion, 106-115
Historicalness, 18-19, 26-27, 137
History of religions,
and theology, 104-115;
horizon of, 105-106
Hocking, William Ernest, 1, 129
Human development, 56-57;
see also Decline; Progress

Icarus myth, 85
Individuation, 85, 135
Infinite, *see* God; Transcendent; Ultimate
Islam, 3, 123, 137

Jaffe, Aniela, 134
Jesus Christ,
and universality of salvation, 34;
as mediator of God's love, 17, 72-73, 136;
as the crucified, 48, 84-86, 88-91, 134;
doctrine of, 16, 65
Job, 48, 82-83
John, First(I), 72
John, Gospel of, 72
John of the Cross, 129
Johnston, William, 1
Judaism, 3, 67, 123, 137;
and early Christianity, 20
Judgement (third level of consciousness), 29-32, 40
Jung, Carl Gustav, 82-85, 88, 90, 135
Jungian active imagination, 126

Kierkegaard, Soren, 44
Kittegawa, Joseph, 125, 138
Klostermaier, Klaus, 1
Knowledge,
and its validity in various disciplines, 23-24;
belief and transmission of, 52-54

Lamb, Matthew, 27, 126
Language, 108-109;
and specific religious terminology,
67-68;
cross-cultural, 66;
limit, 80-81
Learning,
as self-correcting process, 54
Levels (stages) of consciousness, *see* Conscious operations
Loewe, William, 134
Lonergan, Bernard, *passim*
Love,
distinctive language of, 67-68;
God's, 63-65, 69, 72-73, 89-90, 93-96, 98-100;
non-thematized experience of, 60-61;
self-transcending, 42, 44-45, 49, 57, 118
Loyola, Ignatius, 67
Lynch, William, 126

Mark, Gospel of, 72
Marx, Karl, 8; *see also* Marxism
Marxism, 123; *see also* Marx, Karl
Maslow, Abraham, 61
Mathematics, 23, 36
Matthew, Gospel of, 140
Meaning,
mediation of, 52, 69-70, 80
Metaphysics,
and transcendental method, 37-38, 64, 73-74
Method,
and human knowing, 14, 23-28, 36;
empirical, 14, 34, 36;
transcendental (meta-), *see* Transcendental method
Moore, Charles, 133
Moore, Sebastian, 83-91, 94, 115
Morality, *see* Consciousness (moral)
Mystery, 49, 67-68, 98;
cross as central Christian, 84
Mystic,
understanding and importance of, 42, 48-49, 67, 69-71;
see also Mysticism
Mysticism,
atheistic (Buddhist) and theistic (Christian), 70-71;
see also Mystic
Myth, 80

Nasr, Seyyed Hossein, 133
Neumann, Erich, 80
New Testament,
theologies of, 91
Newman, John Henry, 53
Newton, Isaac, 8
Nikhilananda, Swami, 133
Nirvana, 31

Objectivity,
and illusion of non-involvement, 138;
in self-transcending drive toward truth and value, 43;
meaning of, 24, 46, 71
Otto, Rudolf, 67

Pain and pleasure,
as differentiated from value, 44, 51;
in relation to good and evil, 88
Panikkar, Raimundo, 1, 4-6, 66
Papin, Joseph. 128
Pascal, Blaise, 99
Paul, 18, 20, 93, 136
Perez-Valera, J. Eduardo, 127
Philosophy,
modern, 77;
oversights within, 28
Position(s),
and counter-position(s), 28, 82, 120-121
Prayer, 69, 93
Progress, 54-57
Psyche, *see* Conversion (physic)

Questioning,
and wonder, 43, 45;
as intending the transcendent, 45-49;
as the unfolding of conscious operations, 29;
see also Question(s)
Question(s),
descriptive and value, 106, 109, 138;
evaluative, 110-111;
of truth (knowledge), 15, 29-31;
of ultimate meaning, 45-49;
of value (choice), 15, 31-32;
see also Questioning

Rahner, Karl, 67, 98
Ramakrishna, 5
Redemption,
Christian, 83-91;
freedom and community of, 137
Reformation, 20
Religion,
and science, 34-35, *see also* Consciousness (scientific); Science(s);
and secularism, 126;
and the secular, 6-9, 12, 14-15, 66, 117-119;
importance (fuction) of, 6, 56-57, 93, 118-119;
psychological understanding of, 65-66, 84-86, 90-91;
see also Religions; Religious interiority

Religions,
and social enmity and strife, 126;
distinctiveness of, 92, 136;
encounter among, 3-9, 20-21, 65-66;
features of encounter among, 5-6;
shared dimensions of, 93, 98, 102-103;
stages of encounter among, 4-5;
see also Religion; Religious interiority
Religious experience, *see* Religious interiority
Religious interiority,
and decisional level of consciousness, 31-32;
and psychic conversion, 80-91;
and self-transcending horizon(s) of truth, value, ultimacy, 41-49;
as embodied, 108;
as foundational, 10-21, 59-78, 93-94;
objectification of, 61-62, 69-71, 100, 122;
see also Religion; Religions
Renaissance, 14
Ricoeur, Paul, 75
Robinson, John-David, 125, 133
Rogers, Carl, 13
Roman Catholic tradition,
and dialogue among religions, 3;
and doctrines, 16, 64;
and historical transitions of Christianity, 95-96;
and modern consciousness, 8-9;
in relation to universal and particular horizon of faith, 97, 100;
see also Theology (Catholic)
Romans, 48, 64, 72, 93, 133, 139

Salvation, *see* Redemption
Samartha, S. J., 125
Scheler, Max, 80
Scholasticism,
intellectual and theological shift from, 17-18, 37
Science(s),
and human knowing, 36-37, 53-54;
and modernity, 117-118;
see also Consciousness (scientific); Religion (and science)
Scripture, (Christian), 72-73;
see separate listings for individual books
Second Vatican Council (Vatican II), 3, 97
Secularism, 8, 6, 126;
see also Religion (and secularism)
Secularization, 7-8;
see also Religion (and the secular)

Selfhood,
  development of, 39-40, 117-118
Self-transcendence,
  and ego-transcendence, 82;
  and human authenticity, 73;
  and self-inflation, 83, 85;
  and the contemporary world, 6;
  as core to religion, 93-94;
  dialectical character and precariousness of, 44, 102-103, 121;
  in relation to evil/sin, 80-91;
  in relation to truth, value, and the transcendent, 41-49;
  religious, 64-65, *see also* Religious interiority;
  see also Authenticity
Simmel, Georg, 95
Sin, 83
  basic, 86-90, 135;
  differentiated from evil, 134;
  see also Alienation
Smith, Wilfred Cantwell, 97, 103, 105, 115, 138
Socrates, 18
Soul,
  medieval account of, 74
Spiritual direction, 13, 17
Spirituality, *see* Religious interiority
Stark, Claude, 126
Structure,
  infra- and supra-, 30, 122
Subject,
  and communal development, 52-57;
  and conscious operations, 29-36, 38-41;
  and desire for God, 45-49;
  and psyche, 80-82;
  and selfhood, 39-40;
  and self-transcendence, 41-45, 49-51;
  as datum of consciousness, 74;
  as method (recovery of), 12-13, 23-58, 117-122;
  in scientific knowing, 36-37, 117-119;
  modern turn to, 18-19, 77, 115
Subjectivity, *see* Subject
Suzuki, Daisetz, 133
Swartz, Benjamin, 138
Symbol, 80-81, 97, 108
System (systematization), 18-19

Taoism, 137
Taylor, J. B., 125
Theologians(s),
  and historical consciousness, 120, 140;
  and history of religions, 98, 104-115;
  and personal synthesis of faith, 108;
  and recovery of subjectivity, 40-41, 58;
  and religious interiority, 16-17, 76;
  as member of a faith-community, 107-110, 121;
  as method, 26-27;
  focus upon, 3;
  personal conversion of, 82, 120-122;
  see also Theology
Theology,
  and claim to universality, 83;
  and history of religions, 104-115;
  Catholic, 8-9, 76;
  Christian, 1-2, 8-9, 14, 34, 76;
  foundational, 1-2, 7, 16-21, 34-35, 59, 64-66, 74-75, 76, 81, 83, 122-123;
  general and specific categories of, 63-66, 131;
  horizon of, 107-110;
  Lonergan's placement of, 37, 119-120;
  moral, 18;
  mystical (spiritual), 18, 74-75;
  negative, 67;
  Protestant, 8-9;
  relevance of, 7;
  Systematic, 72, 74;
  see also Theologian
Theology of religions, *see* Theology (foundational)
Therapy,
  for the theologian, 10-15;
  intentionality (interiority), 10-15;
  psychological, 11-13
Thomistic synthesis, 8; *see also* Aquinus, Thomas
Tillich, Paul, 67
Transcendent,
  and evil, 86-90;
  and symbolic expression, 80;
  as supreme value, 50-51;
  as truth and value, 41-45;
  openness (orientation) to, 4, 41-51, 60, 62, 75-76, 99, 121-122;
  otherness of, 82-83, 85;
  see also God; Ultimate
Transcendental imperatives, 28, 54, 58
Transcendental (Meta-) method,
  and accumulation of knowledge, 36;
  and classical metaphysics, 37-38;
  as cross-cultural (universal), 33-36, 62-63;
  as foundational, 23-28, 36, 37-38;
  as heuristic, 36;
  intent and form of, 62-63;
  unrevisability of, 33-36, 128

Truth,
intending of (desire for), 40, 41-45, 73, 93;
questions of, 15, 29-31;
transcendental notion of, 41-45, 73, 128

Ultimate,
openness (orientation) to, 44-45, 49, 56, 60-61, 69-70, 80-81, 108, 118, 121; *see also* God; Transcendent

Understanding (second level of consciousness), 29-32, 39-40

Wach, Joachim, 105, 125, 130, 138

West,
and applicability of transcendental method, 33-34, 62-63;
and language of love, 68;
and mystics, 70;
and secularization, 7-8, 14;
and turn to the subject, 18-19, 77, 115;
and understanding of the 'spiritual', 76;
cultural context of, 20;
psychosis of, 12;
scholarship within, 104

Whitehead, Alfred North, 131
Whitson, Robley, 1
Widengren, George, 134
Word, 137;
inner and outer, 94-96

Value,
and economics, 139;
and feeling(s), 49-51;
and satisfactions, 44, 51, 81;
as consequent upon love, 99;
ascending classes of, 51;
finite, 76;
inheritance and assessment of, 113-114;
intending of (desire for), 38, 40, 41-45, 73, 93;
questions of, 15, 31-32;
transcendental notion of, 41-45, 73, 127;
versus vacuum of evil, 86;
see also Consciousness (moral)

Yoga, 20, 127

Zoroastrian Mazdaism, 137